GACE

Birth Through Kindergarten Practice Questions

Mometrix
TEST PREPARATION

DEAR FUTURE EXAM SUCCESS STORY

First of all, **THANK YOU** for purchasing Mometrix study materials!

Second, congratulations! You are one of the few determined test-takers who are committed to doing whatever it takes to excel on your exam. **You have come to the right place.** We developed these study materials with one goal in mind: to deliver you the information you need in a format that's concise and easy to use.

In addition to optimizing your guide for the content of the test, we've outlined our recommended steps for breaking down the preparation process into small, attainable goals so you can make sure you stay on track.

We've also analyzed the entire test-taking process, identifying the most common pitfalls and showing how you can overcome them and be ready for any curveball the test throws you.

Standardized testing is one of the biggest obstacles on your road to success, which only increases the importance of doing well in the high-pressure, high-stakes environment of test day. Your results on this test could have a significant impact on your future, and this guide provides the information and practical advice to help you achieve your full potential on test day.

Your success is our success

We would love to hear from you! If you would like to share the story of your exam success or if you have any questions or comments in regard to our products, please contact us at **800-673-8175** or **support@mometrix.com**.

Thanks again for your business and we wish you continued success!

Sincerely,
The Mometrix Test Preparation Team

Need more help? Check out our flashcards at:
http://mometrixflashcards.com/GACE

Written and edited by the Mometrix Exam Secrets Test Prep Team
Printed in the United States of America

TABLE OF CONTENTS

PRACTICE TEST #1 1
EARLY CHILDHOOD DEVELOPMENT AND LEARNING 1
CONTENT KNOWLEDGE AND RESPONSIVE TEACHING STRATEGIES 8
PROFESSIONALISM AND COLLABORATIVE PARTNERSHIPS 14
ANSWER KEY AND EXPLANATIONS FOR TEST #1 19
EARLY CHILDHOOD DEVELOPMENT AND LEARNING 19
CONTENT KNOWLEDGE AND RESPONSIVE TEACHING STRATEGIES 25
PROFESSIONALISM AND COLLABORATIVE PARTNERSHIPS 31
PRACTICE TEST #2 35
EARLY CHILDHOOD DEVELOPMENT AND LEARNING 35
CONTENT KNOWLEDGE AND RESPONSIVE TEACHING STRATEGIES 41
PROFESSIONALISM AND COLLABORATIVE PARTNERSHIPS 48
ANSWER KEY AND EXPLANATIONS FOR TEST #2 52
EARLY CHILDHOOD DEVELOPMENT AND LEARNING 52
CONTENT KNOWLEDGE AND RESPONSIVE TEACHING STRATEGIES 58
PROFESSIONALISM AND COLLABORATIVE PARTNERSHIPS 65

Practice Test #1

Early Childhood Development and Learning

1. In Piaget's theory of cognitive development, which stages occur during early childhood, i.e., from birth to the age of eight years?

a. Sensorimotor, preoperational, concrete operational
b. Preoperational, concrete operational, formal operational
c. Sensorimotor, preoperational, formal operational
d. Trust vs. Mistrust, Iniative vs. Guilt, Industry vs. Inferiority

2. As young children develop speech, which of the following examples of normal phonological processes typically disappears at the latest age?

a. Pronouncing "sleep" as "teep"
b. Pronouncing "juice" as "goose"
c. Pronouncing "thinks" as "tinks"
d. Pronouncing "pig" as "pick"/"big"

3. Which of these is a correct definition of test-retest reliability?

a. An instrument gives the same results for the same child at the same time and setting by different persons.
b. An instrument's individual items correlate highly with one another and with the overall instrument's score.
c. An instrument includes individual items that cover the entire range of the content area that it claims to test.
d. An instrument gets the same results when given twice or more to the same child within a short time period.

4. An adult has two identically sized and shaped containers holding identical amounts of liquid. S/he pours the same amount from each container into a short, wide glass and a tall, thin glass as a seven-year-old watches. The adult asks the child which glass holds more. The child answers, "They both hold the same amount; I just saw you pour the same amount into each glass." This child demonstrates which ability according to Piaget's theory of cognitive development?

a. Centration of property
b. Permanence of objects
c. Conservation of volume
d. Egocentrism of thought

5. How much usable play space at a minimum do experts recommend per child for indoor and outdoor early childhood learning environments?

a. At least 35 sq. ft. indoors and 75 sq. ft. outdoors
b. At least 25 sq. ft. indoors and 50 sq. ft. outdoors
c. At least 50 sq. ft. indoors and 100 sq. ft. outside
d. At least 45 sq. ft. indoors and 85 sq. ft. outdoors

6. Which statement is true about different screening and assessment instruments that can be used by educational programs for testing young children?

a. These instruments are all comprehensive in assessing multiple domains.
b. There are some instruments focusing on only one facet within a domain.
c. Some instruments focus on a single domain but not on parts of domains.
d. Tests measure developmental domains but not risk or resiliency factors.

7. Which kind of informal assessment can provide the most continuity in recording a pre-K child's progress in a given area or domain?

a. Running records
b. Anecdotal records
c. Portfolio assessments
d. Observational checklists

8. When a child's parents divorce and the father moves out, the child believes it is his fault for saying, "I hate you, go away!" to his father. This belief most illustrates which phenomenon as defined by Piaget?

a. Magical thinking
b. Animistic thinking
c. Symbolic thinking
d. Deductive thinking

9. Which of these is most advisable when designing management plans for common EC behaviors?

a. Once implemented, a plan should never be altered.
b. The most effective plans are difficult to implement.
c. The plan should be complex to cover all possibilities.
d. Recording progress enables effective management.

10. On their way to the "correct" stage of spelling development, in which of the other four stages are children most likely to use invented spellings?

a. Phonetic
b. Transitional
c. Semiphonetic
d. Precommunicative

11. During a task, a toddler throws a tantrum in an effort to get attention from an adult. Which of the following responses would be a consequence that would decrease the probability of repeated tantrums?

a. Ignore the tantrum.
b. Provide task scaffolding.
c. Make a task analysis.
d. Give encouragement.

12. In which of the six stages of art growth and development do children begin to develop a visual schema?

a. Scribble
b. Preschematic
c. Schematic
d. Dawning Realism

13. Which of the following most represents expert guidelines for how much of a young child's speech should be comprehensible to strangers at different ages?

a. Strangers generally can comprehend only about 10% of a child's speech at 1 year.
b. Strangers generally find about 25% of a 2-year-old child's speech to be intelligible.
c. Strangers can usually understand everything a child is saying by the age of 3 years.
d. Strangers will likely not understand everything a child says until s/he is 4 years old.

14. According to Piaget's theory, in what age range do children begin representing things with symbols?

a. Between birth and 6 months
b. Between 6 and 12 months
c. Between 12 and 18 months
d. Between 18 and 24 months

15. Which of these would apply to a test of EC social-emotional development with high content validity?

a. A screening test screens for a child's interactions with caregivers and not those with the child's peers.
b. The test includes items that sample all major aspects of early childhood social-emotional development.
c. A screening test screens for a child's social skills and does not screen for his/her communication skills.
d. A screening test screens for a child's levels of attention and does not screen for his/her initiating play.

16. Which of the following adult practices reflects an understanding of the Anal stage of Freud's theory of psychosexual development?

a. Understanding babies need safe, sanitary things to put in their mouths
b. Understanding the willfulness and stubbornness of behavior in toddlers
c. Understanding preschoolers' focusing on one parent, then on the other
d. Understanding why school children focus on friends more than parents

17. Which of these is accurate regarding individual observations a teacher could make for informal assessments of students in pre-K classes?

a. Teachers would not use a checklist to conduct individual informal assessments.
b. Teachers might keep running records, but should not utilize anecdotal records.
c. Teachers cannot assemble portfolio assessments of children's work for these.
d. Teachers can fill out a chart of various domains with child strengths and needs.

18. Of the following, which is true of Siegfried Engelmann's contributions to early childhood education?

a. The Bereiter-Engelmann Preschool Program tested teaching methods with affluent college faculty's children.
b. Engelmann demonstrated that Piaget's conservation of liquid volume did not depend only on a child's stage.
c. The philosophy and methodology of Direct Instruction were developed by somebody other than Engelmann.
d. Engelmann's research into curriculum and instruction excluded the study of children who had any disabilities.

19. Regarding paper-and-pencil reports for adults to provide screening and assessment of young children, which of these best reflects their characteristics?

a. Such reports must be self-administered at respondents' reading levels in their native languages.
b. These surveys or questionnaires must not be read to respondents even by trained interviewers.
c. Self-reporting instruments have the advantage that they usually take shorter times to complete.
d. ECE program personnel need relatively little training to administer, score, and interpret reports.

20. Which of the following actions represents the use of a fine motor skill?

a. Reaching for a pen
b. Picking up a crayon
c. Sitting down on a chair
d. Standing up from a seat

21. One ECE student's parents want to know if their child is gifted. Another student's parents want to know if their child has a developmental disability. A third student's parents want to know how well their child is mastering all areas of development. A fourth student's parents want to know if and how their child's mastery levels may have changed since last year. What kinds of tests should the educators give the children to answer these parents' questions?

a. Norm-referenced tests for the first and third children, criterion-referenced for the second and fourth children
b. Norm-referenced tests for the first two children, and criterion-referenced tests for the other two children
c. Criterion-referenced tests for the first two children, and norm-referenced tests for the other two children
d. Criterion-referenced tests for the first and third children, norm-referenced for the second and fourth children

22. The minimum amount of outdoor space recommended should be _____ the minimum amount of indoor space recommended for EC learning environments.

a. Over three times
b. Under two times
c. More than twice
d. Exactly two times

23. Which of the following statements is most accurate regarding inter-rater reliability of a screening or assessment instrument used in ECE settings?

a. With tests using unstructured interviews, structured tasks, or observations, rater differences are normal.
b. The test is unreliable if one rater scores a child with possible developmental delay and another as normal.
c. When different assessors observe a child at different times or settings, different results show unreliability.
d. Inter-rater reliability means an instrument measures different constructs depending on the administrator.

24. When can normally developing children typically combine four or more words into sentences?

a. Around 1–2 years old
b. Around 2–3 years old
c. Around 3–4 years old
d. Around 4–5 years old

25. Which of the following is accurate regarding the normal growth of children's brains?

a. Children's brains typically undergo a growth spurt around the age of 3 years.
b. The growth rate of children's brains slows significantly between 7 and 8 years.
c. By the age of 3 years, children's brains have attained 90% of their adult sizes.
d. The majority of children's brain growth has happened by the age of 4½ years.

26. At which ages do normally developing children typically recognize spoken words they hear that name familiar objects, questions, and requests?

a. Around 4–6 months
b. About 7–12 months
c. Around 0–3 months
d. From 12–24 months

27. In self-concept development, which of these is NOT one of the types of Self to develop in early childhood?

a. The Categorical Self
b. The Remembered Self
c. The Inner Self
d. The Outer Self

28. Of Freud's five stages of psychosexual development, which one falls entirely outside of the early childhood years?

a. Genital
b. Latency
c. Phallic
d. Anal

29. Research has found that 75% of children can accurately articulate which of the following speech sounds at the youngest age?

a. The initial "sh" sound in "shut"
b. The initial "v" sound in "voices"
c. The initial "r" sound in "radios"
d. The initial "th" sound in "think"

30. A young child remarks, "The sun burned my skin, because he's mad at me." This best illustrates which cognitive characteristic according to Piaget?

a. Magical thinking
b. Animistic thinking
c. Centrate thinking
d. Symbolic thinking

31. Of the following activities, which is/are typical of a normally developing one-year-old baby?

a. Hold an object in each hand to compare
b. Pick up small objects and stack them up
c. Nest things or drop them into containers
d. One-year-olds can normally do all these.

32. Which of the following does Lev Vygotsky's Zone of Proximal Development represent?

a. The distance between a learner's being in one cognitive developmental stage or the next
b. The distance between the learner's ability and the ability of a More Knowledgeable Other
c. The distance between learner externalized, audible and internalized, mental inner speech
d. The distance between a learner's actual development and learner potential development

33. Which of the following is true regarding development in early childhood?

a. Young children tend to use speech more than physical aggression during conflict.
b. Young children develop and apply motor skills before verbal skills.
c. Young children often know constructive management of strong emotion.
d. Young children learn social skills directly rather than with puppets.

34. In Murray Bowen's Family Systems Theory, what is accurate regarding the relationship pattern he called Impairment of One or More Children?

a. The parents' perception of the child(ren) is negative.
b. The parents' perception of the child(ren) is idealized.
c. The child reacts by reciprocating greater parent focus.
d. Reciprocal focus increases child differentiation of self.

35. Which of the following applies to concurrent validity of screening and assessment instruments used with EC populations?

a. The authors of a new intelligence test have confidence in its statistical strength rather than comparison.
b. The authors of a new intelligence test have compared its results with the Stanford-Binet and the WPPSI.
c. EC educators have a new intelligence test with very different results than Stanford-Binet or than WPPSI.
d. EC educators have a new intelligence test and cannot compare it to tests with prior established validity.

36. Of the following, which can babies typically do from birth?

a. Recognize photos and mirror images as themselves
b. Systematically imitate facial expressions of others
c. Distinguish between internal and external stimuli
d. Systematically reach for and touch seen objects

37. Among six types of play that she identified, which did Mildred Parten find the most socially mature?

a. Independent play
b. Cooperative play
c. Associative play
d. Parallel play

38. Which form of aggression is most common in younger preschoolers up to around 4 years old?

a. Overt aggression
b. Hostile aggression
c. Relational aggression
d. Instrumental aggression

39. In Brown's (1973) Stages of Syntactical and Morphological Development, which of these age ranges is associated with what he designated as Stage I?

a. 12-26 months
b. 15-30 months
c. 24-36 months
d. 27-30 months

40. Which of these has recent research found statistically about influences of ethnic differences on child growth and development?

a. Children in ethnic or racial minority groups are at no more risk for obesity/overweight than others.
b. African-Americans and Latinos have both had double the risk of low birth weights as White infants.
c. Minority group mothers have the same proportion of maternal depression as in other populations.
d. Asthma, related deaths, and risk of poorer treatment are higher for African-Americans than Whites.

Content Knowledge and Responsive Teaching Strategies

41. Which of the following is true about young children's print awareness?

a. Print awareness generally indicates a child is ready to read on his or her own.
b. Print awareness excludes knowing various functions of print.
c. Children develop print awareness before learning to read.
d. It is beyond print awareness to know of books' directionality.

42. Which statement is most accurate about the instructional approach of using scaffolding?

a. It ultimately moves student roles in learning from active to passive.
b. It ultimately requires students to maintain their current knowledge.
c. It ultimately moves learning responsibility from teacher to student.
d. It ultimately moves teacher roles from facilitator/mentor to expert.

43. Which of the following is the most appropriate pre-math learning activity for preschool-aged children?

a. Counting numbers in their heads
b. Counting blocks, beads, or pennies
c. Counting classmates from memory
d. Counting toys through a mental list

44. Which action(s) will teach young children the most about the element of texture in art?

a. They should inspect different textures by looking at them.
b. They should feel different textures by hand without sight.
c. They should produce many different textures themselves.
d. They should do all of these in sequence to learn the most.

45. Which of the following is most effective for teaching pre-math and manipulative skills to preschool children?

a. Giving them solid objects to manipulate physically
b. Giving them information for mental manipulation
c. Giving them math processes to memorize by rote
d. Giving them lessons to listen to while they sit still

46. A group of young children are asked to pour water from a short and wide container into a tall and skinny container. They are then asked whether the amount of water has increased, decreased, or remained the same. Which of the following is primarily being assessed?

a. Conservation
b. Prediction
c. Object permanence
d. Estimation

47. Which activity best demonstrates the use of gross motor skills?

a. Eating
b. Drawing
c. Knot-tying
d. Jumping

48. To communicate effectively with all students in diverse classrooms, which of these is NOT a recommended teacher technique for transitions between topics?

a. Implicit transitions requiring student inferences
b. Verbal signals to the students about transitions
c. Making mini-summaries of the preceding topics
d. Establishing some connections between topics

49. The World Health Organization recommends that between the ages of five and seventeen, children should do which of the following in terms of physical activity?

a. At least three weekly sessions of aerobic activity and one hour daily of weight-bearing activity
b. At least one hour of daily aerobic activity and three weekly sessions of weight-bearing activity
c. At least three days a week for aerobic activity and three days a week of weight-bearing activity
d. At least one hour a day for aerobic activity and one hour per day for weight-bearing activity

50. In the Directed Reading Activity (DRA) approach to reading instruction using basal readers, the first of five steps is the teacher's preparing and motivating students to read, and introducing new concepts and vocabulary words. Which of the following shows the correct sequence of the other four steps?

a. Guided silent reading; comprehension discussion; reading aloud; workbook activities
b. Reading aloud; comprehension discussion; workbook activities; guided silent reading
c. Comprehension discussion; workbook activities; guided silent reading; reading aloud
d. Workbook activities; reading aloud; guided silent reading, comprehension discussion

51. Which of the following can preschool children learn in lessons about the element of color in art?

a. The names of different colors
b. Skills of sensory discrimination
c. Children can learn all of these
d. Skills for making classifications

52. Hands-on, experiential learning activities can further adolescent cognitive and psychosocial development. Which result of these activities is most likely to help preadolescents and younger adolescents resolve the conflict of Industry vs. Inferiority?

a. Transitioning from concrete to abstract thought
b. Having experiences of success in school activity
c. Forming future action plans they find satisfying
d. Transitioning from intuitive to logical reasoning

53. A preschool teacher has children lie down on butcher paper in whatever body positions they choose. The teacher outlines the children's body contours with a marker and has the children personalize them using various drawing tools. This activity best illustrates instruction in which element of visual art?

a. Color
b. Shape
c. Light
d. Line

54. When preschool teachers provide activities to develop social skills, what is true about some necessary skills that young children should and can learn?

a. Young children learn to verbalize what they want in cooperative activities.
b. Preschool children are too egocentric to learn to have empathy for others.
c. Assigning collaborative projects will not teach preschoolers to cooperate.
d. Preschool children are not yet cognitively able to learn how to take turns.

55. What have some researchers found about physical exercise relative to school performance?

a. Children who sit more can focus attention better than those who are more active.
b. Children who are more physically active do better on standardized academic tests.
c. Children who study more have better working memory than more active children.
d. Children who exercise more do not show as good problem-solving skills as others.

56. Which of these is most relevant to EC aesthetic learning activities about texture?

a. To focus on texture, children should feel but not see things.
b. Such activities pertain to art but do not involve vocabulary.
c. These enhance children's skills in symbolic representation.
d. Symbolic representation is an ability beyond preschool age.

57. A prekindergarten teacher uses a combination of verbal cues and nonverbal gestures to signal various transitions in the classroom throughout the school day. This strategy is beneficial in developing students' speaking and listening skills because it:

a. Provides multiple means of understanding
b. Aligns communication with students' developmental levels
c. Demonstrates that communication occurs in a variety of ways
d. Strengthens their understanding of parts of speech and types of sentences

58. Each week, a kindergarten teacher assigns a different student to be the class weather reporter. This student looks outside and describes the weather for the rest of the class. Afterward, the teacher records the student's daily report on a class weather chart. These activities encourage students to do which of the following?

a. Make observations about their environment to identify patterns and make predictions
b. Identify the effects of climate change on daily weather patterns
c. Predict how animals will adapt to changes in temperature
d. Select appropriate articles of clothing for each type of weather

59. Which of the following teacher actions is most effective for fostering greater depth of preschoolers' comprehension of word meanings?

a. Focusing on one definition for a new vocabulary word
b. Introducing new concepts separately from new words
c. Limiting added information to simplify comprehension
d. Giving multiple definitions and examples of new words

60. A child in a preschool learning center likes to sort rocks by their colors. Which of the following teacher practices best represents an emphasis on building the child's problem-solving skills?

a. The teacher asks afterward how else he or she could sort the rocks.
b. The teacher explains to the child that he or she is classifying the rocks.
c. The teacher asks the child which way he or she is sorting rocks.
d. The teacher leaves the students to sorting without intervening.

61. One of the most important factors influencing the quality of learning and development among young children is:

a. Background knowledge and experiences
b. Adequate health and nutrition
c. Intrinsic motivation
d. Parental involvement in the education program

62. Which statement is true about how teachers can help motivate young children to write?

a. Enthusiasm is sustained by diverse writing activities and examples of a variety of writing.
b. Providing children "fun" writing activities will prevent them from taking writing seriously.
c. Making deliberate transcribing errors as children dictate will only give them wrong ideas.
d. Young children should take turns writing an entire class newsletter rather than only parts.

63. Which of the following would be most useful to help young children understand how to organize information?

a. A calendar showing children's daily and/or weekly activity plans
b. A statistical table showing different group rates of achievement
c. A line graph showing daily or weekly differences in attendance
d. A weather forecast showing the chances it will snow that week

64. According to Piaget's theory of cognitive development, how do very young children approach the ideas of part-whole and fractions?

a. They typically think several pieces of an apple equal more fruit than one whole apple.
b. They typically understand that pieces are parts of a whole even at the youngest ages.
c. They typically recognize fractions as parts of a whole if they can use concrete objects.
d. They typically see wholes as more than parts, but not how many parts make a whole.

65. A prekindergarten teacher is leading an activity in which students use discarded items, such as tissue boxes, paper towel rolls, and egg cartons, to create art projects. This teacher is establishing a foundation for understanding which of the following environmental concepts?

a. Recycling as a form of waste management
b. The difference between renewable and nonrenewable resources
c. Ways in which litter contributes to pollution
d. How to distinguish between recyclable and nonrecyclable items

66. What is true about facilitating young children's early development of measurement skills?

a. Adults should discourage children from using their own personal measuring units.
b. Adults should teach children standardized measurement units in isolated lessons.
c. Adults should explain measuring to children when demonstrating everyday tasks.
d. Adults should ask children to participate in everyday tasks and discuss measuring.

67. A prekindergarten teacher uses daily circle time for reading aloud to students. When introducing new vocabulary words from a text, the teacher pauses to explain their meaning, and adds them to the class word wall with corresponding pictures. After each read-aloud, the teacher also asks students to discuss their favorite parts of the story. By implementing these strategies, the teacher demonstrates understanding of which of the following?

a. Individual differences in developmental levels among young children
b. The role of receptive and expressive language in literacy development
c. Interventions for supporting literacy development in struggling students
d. The importance of differentiating instruction to align with individual students' needs

68. Which of the following strategies would likely be most effective in teaching prekindergarten students to listen responsively to directions?

a. Implementing listening games with simple multi-step directions
b. Choral reading poems, rhymes, and familiar stories
c. Changing intonation when giving verbal directions
d. Using gestures, body language, and visual cues

69. One of the easiest tasks for phonological awareness is:

a. Replacing sounds to make new words
b. Hearing rhyming sounds within words
c. Isolating and classifying word sounds
d. Blending and/or separation of sounds

70. A child who understands that the word *books* means two or more while *book* means one is demonstrating an understanding of:

a. Phonology
b. Morphology
c. Syntax
d. Semantics

71. What is true about children's books that educators term "predictable books"?

a. They feature unoriginal plots.
b. They enable immediate participation and practice.
c. They challenge children's abilities to decode complex sentences.
d. They are simple novels that serve as a bridge between picture books and books targeted toward adolescents.

72. What is true about the sequence that teachers should use for phonics instruction with young children?

a. Teachers should introduce letters with similar sounds in separate lessons.
b. Teachers should introduce stop consonants before continuous consonants.
c. Teachers should introduce letters that look similar during the same lesson.
d. Teachers should introduce low-utility before high-utility letters and sounds.

73. To help young children practice the collection, organization, and display of data, which of the following activities would be most relevant?

a. A teacher lets children choose differently shaped stickers and identify what those shapes are
b. A teacher lets children choose differently colored stickers and guess numbers of colors picked
c. A teacher lets children choose differently colored stickers and match them to colors on a chart
d. A teacher lets children choose differently colored stickers as cumulative rewards toward prizes

74. During unstructured play time, a kindergarten teacher asks a group of students in the block area to arrange the blocks from largest to smallest. This is likely intended to promote students' early development of which of the following foundational skills related to mathematics?

a. Measurement
b. Geometric awareness
c. Pattern recognition
d. Sequencing

75. Of these instructional models, which one involves the most variation in teacher roles?

a. Traditional teacher-centered models
b. Progressive student-centered models
c. Small-group cooperative learning models
d. Differentiated instruction models

76. Which statement is most accurate regarding young students' reading comprehension?

a. Students missing main ideas while noticing details are more likely to have comprehension issues.
b. Missing either the main ideas or the details of the text signifies comprehension problems.
c. Students who cannot repeat any details but get the main idea have good comprehension.
d. If a student gets the main ideas, the ability to retell logical event sequences is immaterial.

77. What statement is accurate regarding integrated ECE curricula using thematic units?

a. Organizing by themes addresses groups rather than individual child differences.
b. Organizing by themes affords many hands-on learning activities for preschoolers.
c. Organizing by themes requires assessments other than portfolio or performance.
d. Organizing by themes makes learning meaningful but excludes any benchmarks.

78. A kindergarten teacher wants to promote students' ability to retell a fictional story in sequential order. Which of the following activities would be most effective in achieving this goal with students of this age group?

a. Providing students with a story map to fill out as they read
b. Having students sort events from the story using picture cards
c. Modeling how to identify transitional words and phrases in the text
d. Having students arrange sentences from the story in the order in which they happened

79. Which of the following strategies would best demonstrate to prekindergarten students the purpose and use of a printed book?

a. Taking a class trip to the school library
b. Asking students to bring in their favorite book from home
c. Modeling how to hold a book, turn pages, read from left to right, and pointing out key characteristics
d. Incorporating time for reading aloud into the school day

80. Of the following statements, which is true regarding instructional techniques relative to individual student differences?

a. Assigning small groups is best for giving both re-teaching and enrichment to students.
b. Assigning small groups is best for re-teaching skills or concepts to struggling students.
c. Assigning small groups is best for offering enrichment activities to advanced students.
d. Assigning small groups is best for only classes where levels are equal among students.

Professionalism and Collaborative Partnerships

81. Among the following, which is correct regarding legal regulations regarding record confidentiality in early childhood education (ECE) settings?

a. FERPA mandates student records confidentiality for every ECE program/facility/agency existing in the USA.
b. The special education laws of each US state supersede IDEA for confidentiality of disabled student records.
c. Laws penalize ECE employees for releasing records but require them to report suspected child abuse or neglect.
d. Laws require ECE employees to report suspected abuse/neglect and protect those employees for doing so.

82. Which of the following best reflects actions that enable and support positive interactions among adults within ECE settings?

a. EC educators should respect student privacy by not sharing anecdotal records and observations with colleagues.
b. Communicating to other adults about children and families is not positive interaction because of confidentiality.
c. EC educators should share their observations and records on students, but should not plan instruction together.
d. EC educators use problem-solving activities and dialogues to discern how to enhance child learning experiences.

83. In a hypothetical scenario, an EC teacher sees injuries to a child in her class. She also has observed that this child's mother has a new boyfriend; behaves fearfully; and is evasive with the teacher's questions. Then the child tells this teacher that this new boyfriend hurt the child. Which description of the teacher's response would best meet legal responsibilities for a professional in the ECE setting?

a. The teacher feels sorry for the mother and her situation and does not report suspicions she cannot prove.
b. The teacher knows the mother depends on the boyfriend financially and emotionally and does not report.
c. The teacher reports her suspicions because the law requiring it was made to stop violence against children.
d. The teacher reports her suspicions regardless because the law requires it and penalizes her for not doing it.

84. A kindergarten teacher strives to create positive, collaborative relationships with students' families. To achieve this, the teacher utilizes multiple methods of communication, including a class website, a paper-based newsletter, phone calls, emails, and in-person conferences. Which of the following best describes how this helps establish and maintain such relationships?

a. Using cross-culturally competent communication practices
b. Meeting the communication needs of all students' families
c. Documenting interactions for use in family conferences
d. Gaining insight into students' backgrounds, experiences, and individual learning needs

85. A prekindergarten teacher maintains an online blog to document and share teaching experiences, instructional strategies, and classroom activities. The teacher wants to post photos of a recent activity her students completed in class. Before posting the photos, which of the following measures must the teacher take in order to protect students' right to privacy?

a. Request permission from the school administration to create the post
b. Remove students' faces from the photos
c. Inform students' families that pictures of a classroom activity will be posted online
d. Ensure that the photos do not include students' personally identifiable information

86. A student's parents recently attended a conference with their child's teacher. While the teacher was professional, the overall tone of the conference was rigid, as he began by highlighting the student's missing assignments and academic weaknesses. Which of the following would have been a more effective approach in encouraging these parents to share information that would enhance their child's learning experience?

a. Inviting the grade-level administrator to attend the conference
b. Allowing the student to attend the conference
c. Creating a welcoming atmosphere and beginning with positive remarks about the student
d. Sending the parents an outline of topics to be covered prior to the conference

87. Which of the following is true regarding the inclusion of families in early childhood education?

a. The family use of parenting skills is none of the educator's business.
b. One-way educator communication to families periodically is enough.
c. Educators should acknowledge parents' integral role in child learning.
d. School staff should make parents feel welcome but not ask for their help.

88. What is correct about how teachers are evaluated in performance appraisal systems?

a. Professional communication is not an appraised topic.
b. Professional development for the teacher is included.
c. Compliance with policies and procedures for operations is not evaluated.
d. Only improvement for identified students is assessed.

89. Which of the following is correct regarding parents and education?

a. The way parents converse has no effect on their children's classroom communications.
b. Educators need not be as concerned about parent expectations as school expectations.
c. Educators can help parents pursue ESL and GED programs, which support their children.
d. Referring students' parents to community resources is outside the scope for educators.

90. Which statement related to teacher professional development (PD) goals and processes is most accurate?

a. US states all certify/license teachers with BA/BS degrees and do not require a master's degree.
b. Teachers earn the same licensure regardless of the PD goals of individual US states.
c. Once a teacher has an advanced graduate degree, there is no need for further goals.
d. PD goals can include reading professional literature as well as taking specific courses.

91. Which of the following is true about teacher appraisals?

a. They are conducted based on federal guidelines.
b. They are used primarily to ensure teacher attendance.
c. They are usually conducted by third-party evaluators.
d. They are generally regulated at the local level.

92. What is applicable regarding teacher professional development (PD) routes?

a. Once hired, teachers usually only get PD via professional organizations.
b. Working teachers do not have the time to attend graduate PD courses.
c. Teachers use PD only to get higher degrees/certificates in the same subject.
d. Many teachers learn additional subjects and/or specialties through PD.

93. Regarding cultural influences on parental childcare and education preferences, which result is true?

a. Hispanic families in the US are found to use preschool centers more.
b. Hispanic families in the US are found to prefer home/family settings.
c. Caucasian and Hispanic families in the US use center and home care equally.
d. Caucasian families in the US are likely to prefer family/home settings.

94. What statement is most accurate about medical emergencies and treatment in ECE settings?

a. ECE staff should always call an ambulance in all emergencies rather than requesting transportation from parents.
b. ECE administrators must designate vehicles and employees for transport when awaiting parents is impossible.
c. ECE administrators should recruit as many staff members as possible to help with medical emergency treatments.
d. ECE staff administrators designated for assistance in emergencies do not necessarily need current first aid training.

95. What statement is most accurate regarding adult interactions in early childhood education practice?

a. Early childhood research includes extensive work on how adult collaboration influences children.
b. Early childhood educators need to use teamwork to foster safe, trustworthy climates for children.
c. Early childhood curriculum models and approaches do not address any interactions among adults.
d. Early childhood professional development and training often cover topics about adult interaction.

96. Among the following, which is true for EC teachers to establish and maintain good communication with parents?

a. When an EC teacher calls each parent during the first two weeks of school, it causes alarm for most parents.
b. It is easier for teachers to call parents later in the school year if issues warrant when they have not first called earlier.
c. Parents learn to expect no communication if teachers publish print/online weekly/monthly class newsletters.
d. Parents perceive teachers sending home parent letters at the beginning of the school year as more available.

97. One important element of school-community partnerships is activities that students, schools, and their communities all mutually value and find meaningful. What accurately represents other important elements?

a. School outreach should enlist community member involvement and support.
b. Means of community member involvement with schools should be standard.
c. Communication between schools and their communities should be unilateral.
d. The concept of community learning centers should only apply outside school.

98. Which of these is true regarding guidelines for ECE programs related to children's non-emergency medical illnesses, chronic conditions, and possible emergencies?

a. When a child gets sick, ECE staff follow the program's health policies and consult with parents about whether the child should leave the facility.
b. Non-emergency medical treatments do not require filed procedures and reports like emergencies do.
c. Doctors and nurses are not authorized to provide routine medical treatment by parent consent forms.
d. Information on chronic medical conditions and treatment directions should be on file, but not posted.

99. Which statement is most accurate about the problems encountered in interactions between American educators and culturally diverse families?

a. The problems are encountered primarily by culturally diverse families.
b. The problems are encountered primarily by the American educators.
c. The problems are encountered equally by the families and educators.
d. The problems are encountered usually quite minimally by either group.

100. The Education Practices Commission can revoke an educator's certificate for which of the following?

a. Pursuing or obtaining certification by fraudulent means
b. Unwittingly failing to report suspected abuse of a child
c. Suspected incompetence for school teaching or duties
d. Conviction of a crime but not pleading guilty to a crime

Answer Key and Explanations for Test #1

Early Childhood Development and Learning

1. A: The sensorimotor stage is from birth to roughly age 2. The preoperational stage occurs from roughly ages 2-7. The concrete operational stage occurs from roughly ages 7-11. Infants to 8-year-olds are typically in one of these stages. The formal operational stage is around the age of 11 years and older. Answer D lists stages from Erikson's model, not Piaget's.

2. C: Pronouncing "thinks" as "tinks" equals articulating a fricative as a stop. This normal phonological process typically disappears when children are about 5 years old. Pronouncing "sleep" as "teep" (A) equals the reduction of a consonant cluster to a single consonant; this typically disappears when children are around 4 years old. Pronouncing "juice" as "goose" (B) equals articulating an affricate (a combination of a stop like /d/ with a fricative like /ʒ/ to form /ʤ/, the "j" sound in "juice") as a stop—in this case, /g/. This normally disappears when a child is about 4½ years old. Pronouncing "pig" as "pick" equals devocalizing the final consonant, while pronouncing "pig" as "big" (D) equals pre-vocalic voicing, i.e., letting the voicing of the vowel sound transfer to a preceding unvoiced consonant like /p/, making it /b/. These normal phonological processes both typically disappear when children are about 3 years old.

3. D: Test-retest reliability means that a test instrument will yield the same results when administered two or more times to the same child within a short period of time. Developmental changes in early childhood occur too rapidly for this to apply if testing is done over a longer time period. Answer choice A is a definition of inter-rater reliability. Answer choice B is a definition of internal consistency reliability. Answer choice C is a definition of content validity.

4. C: This child demonstrates conservation of (liquid) volume by knowing both glasses hold the same amount regardless of their shapes or sizes. Centration of property (A) is what a younger child does in focusing on only one property at a time, e.g. either the height or width of the container but not both. Piaget said centration prevents conservation. Object permanence (B) is the realization babies develop that things still exist even when they cannot see them. Egocentrism (D) is characteristic of the thinking of children in the Preoperational stage, when they cannot see things from another person's perspective but only their own.

5. A: Early childhood education experts recommend providing at least 35 square feet indoors per child and 75 square feet outdoors of usable play space per child for learning environments. Answer B would not provide enough room for typical young children to engage in usual activities and avoid fighting or competing among age groups. Options C and D would be excellent but do not reflect the recommended minimums.

6. B: While some tests are comprehensive, assessing children's development in multiple domains, not all are (A). Some tests focus on a single domain (C), like language or emotional-social development, while others can even focus on one facet within a domain {(B), (C)}, like attachment or temperament within the emotional-social domain of development. In addition to developmental domains, some tests measure risk and resiliency factors (D) that influence developmental delays and disorders.

7. A: Anecdotal records provide valuable information that may not be captured in forms that teachers fill out for other informal assessments, but they are most often reports of occasional events or observations. Portfolio assessments compile children's work products over periods of time, offering first-hand records of progress and cumulative assessments, but they limit evaluation of progress to separate examples created at separate points in time. Observational checklists completed at regular intervals also show progress and/or change over time but only as snapshots of particular moments. Running records are the most continuous of the informal assessments named.

8. A: This example illustrates what Piaget called magical thinking: the belief that what one thinks, feels, or says causes events that happen outside of him/her in the environment. Animistic thinking (B) is attributing human qualities to inanimate objects. Symbolic thinking (C) is using objects/people to represent other objects/people in pretend/make-believe play. Using symbols is also necessary for children to learn the alphabetic principle and phonics in order to read and write. Deductive thinking (D) is the logic whereby one predicts specific instances according to generalized principles; it typically does not fully develop until the stage of Formal Operations and abstract thought, around 11 years and older.

9. D: Once adults have implemented a plan to manage a behavior in an EC setting, they must record the child's progress regularly. By analyzing the records they keep, they can determine which parts of the plan are working and which are not, or whether the entire plan is not working. If they find that a plan is ineffective despite adhering to it consistently for a sufficient time, they can figure out why and then replace it with a new plan more suited to the child, the behavior, and its function. If only parts of the plan are ineffective, it can be revised to change those parts; hence, answer choice A is incorrect. EC staff should begin with plans that are easy to implement, not difficult (B) and are simple, not complex (C).

10. A: The first stage of spelling development is precommunicative (D), when children may use alphabet letters but have no idea these represent speech sounds. In the second, semiphonetic (C) stage, children begin to understand the correspondences of letters to sounds and use basic logic, like spelling "you" as "U" or "why" as "Y." The third stage is the phonetic (A) stage, when children do not necessarily use conventional spelling, but represent every phoneme they hear in a word with a letter or letter group in a systematic and comprehensible way. This is when they are most likely to use invented or phonetic spellings. In the fourth, transitional (B) stage, children begin to use visual instead of auditory spellings.

11. A: The key to decreasing the probability of a behavior's repetition is the behavior's function. In this case, the tantrum was to get attention. Giving any kind of attention would reinforce the behavior (i.e., increase the probability of repeated tantrums). Ignoring the behavior is the only choice that does not provide attention. If the tantrum's function had instead been to express frustration with the task, then the adult could provide support for performing it; break the task down into smaller, more manageable steps, or encourage the child to persevere at the task.

12. B: During the Preschematic stage, around the ages of 4–6 years, children begin to develop a visual schema. In the Scribble (A) stage, which precedes the Preschematic, children first make uncontrolled scribbles, then controlled scribbles, and then name what their scribbles represent. In the Schematic (C) stage, around 7–9 years of age, following the Preschematic, children draw pictures more accurately reflective of real physical proportions, body parts, features, and colors. In the stage of Dawning Realism (D), around the ages of 9–11 years, children make increasingly representational drawings.

13. D: Familiarity enables parents to understand their young children's speech better when the children are younger than when strangers can understand the same proportions of their speech. According to a number of experts, strangers can usually understand about 25% of a 1-year-old's speech, not 10% (A). Of 2-year-old children's speech, about 50% is typically intelligible to strangers, not 25% (B). Whereas parents may understand all or most of what their 3-year-olds say, strangers usually understand only about 75% of it, not everything (C). Strangers will not understand everything uttered by young children until they are around 4 years old (D).

14. D: Piaget theorized that children begin to use symbols to represent other things around the ages of 18–24 months. This is evident in their pretend play, when they might use a broom to represent a horse or a guitar, use a block to represent a phone, or pretend to be adults when playing "House," etc. Children are not typically observed to use symbols this way before 18 months, and not doing so until later than 24 months would represent a cognitive developmental delay.

15. B: Content validity means that a test measures the entire content area it claims to measure, and this broad sampling is what primarily characterizes high content validity. However, if a test to screen for social-emotional development, for example, screens for a child's interactions with caregivers but not with peers (A); or screens for social skills but not communication skills (C); or screens for attention but not for initiation of play (D), the test would have low content validity by not screening for all elements of social-emotional development.

16. B: Understanding babies need to mouth things to learn about the world orally (A) reflects Freud's Oral stage of development. In this stage, Freud said learning is influenced by the oral focus of early nursing activity. Understanding willful and stubborn behavior in toddlers (B) reflects Freud's Anal stage, when they are becoming toilet-trained, learning to control their bodies, and to assert individual will. Understanding why preschoolers first focus on the opposite-sex parent, and later on the same-sex parent (C) reflects Freud's phallic stage. At this time, Freud said about boys, and neo-Freudians added about girls, that they undergo Oedipal and Electra conflicts of unconscious impulses of desiring the opposite-sex parent and wanting to eliminate the same-sex parent as a rival. Children resolve these conflicts by "identification with the aggressor," resolving guilt over unacceptable impulses by emulating same-sex parents. Understanding children's shift of focus from parents to friends when they start school (D) reflects Freud's Latency stage, when psychosexual impulses are buried to permit expanding social and academic experiences.

17. D: One way teachers can use individual observations for informal assessments is to fill out a chart divided into domains like physical development, oral language development, math, emergent reading and writing, science, health, fine arts, technology and media, social studies, social-emotional development, and approaches to learning with one child's strengths and needs in each domain per chart. Another way is to complete a checklist (A). Another is to keep running records, and/or use anecdotal records (B) of children's progress. Teachers can also assemble portfolio assessments of children's work (C) as informal assessments of their learning over time.

18. B: Siegfried Engelmann collaborated with Carl Bereiter in experiments reexamining Piaget's theory of cognitive development. While Piaget had maintained that the ability to conserve liquid volume depended only on the child's level of cognitive development, Engelmann and Bereiter showed that this ability could also be taught to children before they reached the corresponding Piagetian stage. The Bereiter-Engelmann Preschool Program did not test teaching methods with affluent college faculty children (A); Piaget's case studies used such children, but the Bereiter-Engelmann Program demonstrated the effectiveness of intensive instruction for enhancing cognitive skills in disadvantaged preschool-aged children. Engelmann did develop the philosophy and methodology of Direct Instruction (C) through his research into curriculum and instruction, which included children with Down syndrome (D) as well as children from impoverished backgrounds.

19. C: Self-reporting instruments do have the advantage that they usually take fewer than 20 minutes for parents, caregivers, and teachers to complete. *If* they are self-administered, they must be at the respondents' reading levels and in their native language (A); but some of them *can* alternatively be read to respondents by interviewers who are trained in or familiar with the instrument's administration (B). While ECE program personnel need relatively little training to administer these assessments, they may need more training to score and interpret them (D); or in some cases, trained specialists may score and interpret them instead.

20. B: Fine motor skills involve small movements and small muscles, such as of the fingers, wrists, tongue, lips, and toes. An example is picking up a small object like a crayon or a spoon. Gross motor skills involve large movements and large muscles, as of the torso, arms, legs, and feet. Examples include rolling over and crawling as infant developmental milestones; reaching for something (A) with the arms; sitting down (C); standing up (D); and running, jumping, climbing, kicking, throwing, catching, etc.

21. B: Norm-referenced tests compare a student's scores to the scores of a sample of students that are representative of the population for the same age, developmental level, or grade. They show how a student's performance compares to the average and whether that student is achieving significantly above or below the norm. Therefore, to tell parents if their children perform above average and may be gifted or below average and may have developmental disabilities, educators would administer norm-referenced tests. Criterion-referenced tests compare a student's scores to a performance standard for the student's age, developmental level, or grade, which has been pre-determined by educational experts. They show how a student's performance compares to established standards. To tell parents if their children have mastered all areas of development or whether and how children's mastery levels have changed over time, educators would administer criterion-referenced tests.

22. C: ECE experts recommend a minimum of 35 square feet of space indoors and 75 square feet of space outdoors for learning environments. Therefore, the minimum space recommended for outdoor spaces is more than two times the minimum space recommended for indoor spaces. (A) is more than this; (B) and (D) are less.

23. B: If one rater of a test scores a child as possibly having a developmental delay or disorder, and another rater of the same test scores the same child as being within normal developmental limits, this means the test has poor inter-rater reliability and hence is unreliable for identifying the child's actual developmental status. Significant differences, especially with instruments using unstructured interviews, structured tasks, or observations, present problems and are not normal or expected (A). However, when different raters, such as teacher vs. parent, observe a child at different times or settings, like preschool vs. home, rater differences do NOT necessarily show unreliability (C) but are expected, as young children's behaviors can vary by settings and times. Inter-rater reliability means an instrument measures the *same* construct regardless of the administrator, not vice versa (D).

24. C: When children are around 1–2 years old (A), they typically can combine two words into questions and statements. When they are around 2–3 years old (B), they typically can make utterances combining up to three words. Around 3–4 years of age, they typically can combine four or more words. At around 4–5 years old (D), they typically can speak fluently and clearly in long, complex, compound, and complex-compound sentences.

25. D: By around 4 to 4½ years of age, children's brains have normally undergone the majority of their growth. Children's brains typically undergo a growth spurt around the age of 2 years, not 3

(A). The growth rate of children's brains slows significantly between the ages of 5 and 6 years, not 7 and 8 (B). Children's brains have attained 90% of their adult size by the age of 6 years, not 3 (C).

26. B: Babies typically begin turning to look at parents upon hearing their voices, stop crying upon hearing familiar voices, and stop what they are doing to listen to an unfamiliar voice between birth and 3 months of age (C). At around 4–6 months (A) old, babies are typically responsive to the word "no" and to changes in parental tones of voice, as well as to nonvocal sounds. When they are about 7–12 months old, they recognize familiar spoken words for objects, people, questions, and requests (B). Children aged 12–24 months (D) can point to some body parts upon request and to pictures in a book upon hearing them named and can follow simple directions and understand simple questions.

27. D: Three types of Self that develop during early childhood are the Categorical Self (A), a concrete self-concept related to observable, opposing characteristics like girl vs. boy, short vs. tall, good vs. bad, etc.; the Remembered Self (B), which develops with long-term memory, comprises the child's life story, and includes autobiographical memories and things adults have told them; and the Inner Self (C), composed of the child's private feelings, desires, and thoughts. There are only these three types in this classification, which has no such designation as an Outer Self (D).

28. A: Freud associated his fifth, Genital stage of development with the ages of puberty and thereafter and the re-emergence of sexuality. He associated his first, oral stage with infancy and nursing; his second, anal (D) stage with toddlerhood and toilet-training; his third, phallic (C) stage with the preschool years and early discovery of sexuality; and his fourth, latency (B) stage with the elementary school years and repressed sexuality, which is deferred while developing cognitive and social skills takes precedence.

29. A: According to some research studies, 75% of normally developing children could accurately pronounce the "sh" sound in "shut" by the age of 4 years. 75% of children could accurately pronounce the "v" in "voices" (B) by the age of 6 years. 75% of children could accurately pronounce the "r" in "radios" (C) by the age of 5 years. And 75% of children could accurately articulate the "th" in "think" (D) by the age of 8½ years.

30. B: This is an example of animism, i.e. attributing human qualities, thoughts, and feelings to inanimate objects. It is characteristic of Preoperational children. Magical thinking (A), also characteristic of this stage, is the belief that one's thoughts, feelings, or speech causes external environmental events. Centrate thinking (C) or centration, also typical of Preoperational thought, is focusing on only one property of an object at a time. Symbolic thinking (D) develops near the end of the Sensorimotor stage, when children begin to represent objects/people with other objects/people in pretend/make-believe play.

31. D: By the age of one year, normally developing babies can typically hold an object in each hand to look at them comparatively (A), pick up small objects and stack them vertically (B), nest objects inside of other objects, and drop objects into containers (C).

32. D: What Vygotsky termed the Zone of Proximal Development (ZPD) referred to his concept of the distance between the learner's actual development, i.e., what s/he can do independently, and the learner's potential development, i.e., what s/he can do with help/guidance from a More Knowledgeable Other (MKO). Vygotsky's term does NOT refer to distance between the learner's ability and the MKO's ability (b). It does NOT refer to distance between cognitive developmental stages (a); in fact, he disagreed with Piaget's belief that such stages were always the same in nature and sequence because Vygotsky believed these were highly influenced by cultural factors. Given his belief in variance in cognitive development, Vygotsky would not propose a distance between stages. Although Vygotsky did originate the concept and term of inner speech and its progressing from externalized and audible to internalized and mental (c), the ZPD does not refer to inner speech.

33. B: Children's motor skills typically develop sooner than their verbal skills. During conflict, young children are more likely to use physical aggression like kicking, biting, hitting, and pushing/shoving to get what they want rather than using speech (A). Young children also often have trouble self-regulation emotion, so teachers must help them learn how to manage their strong emotions constructively (C). Young children do not learn social skills only directly; teachers can help develop their social skills by demonstrating aggressive vs. proactive behaviors using puppets (D), which preschoolers find entertaining as well as concrete representations of emotions they can understand.

34. C: In describing the parent-child relationship pattern he termed Impairment of One or More Children, Bowen said that the parents have either a negative (A) or idealized (B) perception of the child(ren) with the impairment. Either way, they focus their anxieties on the impaired child(ren). Bowen explained that when parents focus more on a child(ren), the reaction of the child(ren) is to focus reciprocally more on the parents, becoming more reactive than siblings to parental expectations, needs, and attitudes. This mutual excessive focus undermines healthy differentiation of self (D) in the child(ren).

35. B: The Stanford-Binet Intelligence Scales and the WPPSI (Wechsler Preschool and Primary Scales of Intelligence) are both established instruments whose statistical validity and reliability have been proven. Since EC educators have confidence in these tests, a new instrument whose results compare closely to theirs would have high concurrent validity. Having confidence in a test's statistical strength, but without comparison to trusted existing tests, does not represent concurrent validity (A). If the new test gets very different results from established tests (C), this represents a lack of concurrent validity. If educators cannot compare a new test to existing tests for validity (D) or reliability, the new test is not shown to have concurrent validity.

36. C: From birth, infants can tell the difference between their own bodies and the environment around them. They can differentiate between internal stimulation from touching themselves and external stimulation from others touching them. Children typically develop the recognition of photos and mirror images as symbolic representations of themselves (A) by the time they are around two years old. Babies typically develop systematic imitation of others' facial expressions (B), gestures, and other movements around the age of two months. They usually develop the ability of systematically reaching for and touching things they see (D), which requires eye-hand coordination, around the age of four months.

37. B: Parten identified, in order of social maturity, (1) Unoccupied; (2) Independent or Solitary play; (3) Onlooker behavior; (4) Parallel play; (5) Associative play; and (6) Cooperative play. She found playing alone, i.e., Independent play (a) less socially mature; then observing others playing (Onlooker behavior); then playing alongside/near others but separately, i.e., Parallel play (d); then interacting with others playing without coordination or organization, i.e., Associative play (c); and the most socially mature as interacting with others in organized, coordinated play including assigned/assumed roles and interest in both activity and playmates, i.e., Cooperative play (b).

38. D: Instrumental aggression is behavior wherein a child yells, kicks, or hits others to get something they want, usually a toy or other object. It is the most commonly seen form of aggression in early preschoolers through the age of around 4 years, when it often peaks. Hostile aggression is more common in middle preschoolers older than 4 years and involves retaliating against others in return for being wronged or hurt by them. Hostile aggression has two types: overt aggression (more common in boys), wherein they physically hurt others and/or threaten to do so; and relational aggression (more common in girls), wherein they emotionally and/or socially hurt others through circulating hurtful rumors and/or rejecting them socially.

39. A: Brown designated Stage I as typical of children 12 to 26 months old. 15-30 months (B) and 24-36 months (C) are not age ranges used by Brown for the developmental stages he defined. 27-30 months (D) is the age range Brown designated as associated with his Stage II of language development. 31-34 months is the age range Brown associated with his Stage III of language development.

40. D: Recent surveys in the United States have found that African-American children had higher rates of asthma, asthma-related deaths, and higher risk for poorer quality and continuity of care in asthma treatment than White children. Research also has found children in minority groups at higher risk for obesity/overweight (A), as well as low-income children, than other children. Studies have found the risk of low birth weights to be double for African-Americans than Whites; however, Latinos had slightly lower risk of low birth weight than Whites (B). Mothers in minority groups as well as low-income groups have been found to have proportionately higher rates of maternal depression than in other parts of the population (C). Poor mother-child bonding, lower language and reading scores for children, and higher rates of mental health problems including depression in children when they get older are all associated with maternal depression.

Content Knowledge and Responsive Teaching Strategies

41. C: Before they learn to read, children develop print awareness. Print awareness includes knowing the different functions that print serves in different contexts (e.g. in restaurant menus, story books, informational books, directional signs, warning signs, business name signs, etc.) and knowing the directionality of print in books.

42. C: Scaffolding is temporary support that teachers provide to students to enable them to accomplish tasks they cannot yet achieve alone, and which teachers gradually withdraw as students progress toward task/skill mastery. It ultimately moves the student role in learning from passive to active (a); requires students to increase their current knowledge (b); moves the responsibility for learning from the teacher to the student (c); and moves teachers from playing expert roles to facilitator and mentor roles (d).

43. B: Preschool-aged children must have solid, concrete objects they can physically manipulate to understand numerical concepts. They are not yet cognitively able to manipulate information mentally, which is required by all of the other choices.

44. D: To teach young children the most about the element of texture in art, EC teachers can have them inspect various textures visually and discuss their qualities and differences. Then they can offer children boxes or bags with variously textured objects inside and have them describe and differentiate these without seeing them. Then teachers can have children use various implements—child-safe pottery tools, tongue depressors, chopsticks, plastic tableware, small toys, etc.—to produce different textures in clay or plaster and see how many ways they can make the material feel and look. Letting children paint the pieces they create after they have dried reinforces what they have learned about textures, by supplying additional fun and pride in having created visible, tangible products they can keep and show others. Doing all these in sequence teaches children the most about texture through visual, verbal, and tactile modalities, and through observation, communication, comparison, and creation.

45. A: Young children must have concrete things they can see, touch, and manipulate. They are not yet cognitively capable of manipulating information mentally (B). They are not yet able to memorize math processes by rote (C), as older elementary-age children can memorize times tables, etc. They are too young to benefit from "sit still and listen" types of lessons (D).

46. A: Pouring liquid into differently sized and shaped containers is an activity that is easy and fun for young children to do. It helps develop young children's ability to achieve what Piaget termed conservation of liquid volume, which is the understanding that an amount remains the same despite being transferred to a different shape or size of container. Object permanence refers to the understanding that an object still exists even after it goes out of sight. While the children may predict the water will remain the same or estimate the volumes, these are not the primary skills being assessed.

47. D: Jumping, running, climbing, sitting, standing, and walking are activities that demonstrate the use of gross motor skills, which involve the large muscles of the body. Eating with fingers or utensils; drawing; and tying knots are all activities demonstrating the use of fine motor skills, which involve the small muscles of the hands and fingers and eye-hand coordination.

48. A: Experts recommend that for effective communication, teachers make *explicit* transitions between topics by signaling them verbally (B), making mini-summaries of each topic before moving to the next topic (C), and/or establishing the connections between one topic and the next (D). They do NOT recommend leaving transitions between topics implicit for students to infer (A).

49. B: The WHO's recommendations are that young people engage in at least one hour per day of aerobic activity, which strengthens the heart, lungs, and large muscle groups. This makes the cardiovascular and respiratory systems more efficient in the absorption and transportation of oxygen. These recommendations also include at least three sessions a week of weight-bearing activity, which strengthens the bones.

50. A: In the DRA approach, after teacher preparation and motivation of students and introduction of new concepts and vocabulary words, in the second step, students read silently with questions and statements from the teacher guiding their reading. In the third step, teacher and students discuss what they have read to develop student reading comprehension. In the fourth step, students read aloud. They also read answers aloud to questions the teacher has asked; this is called "purposeful rereading." The fifth step involves follow-up activities and practicing that students do using the companion workbooks to the basal readers. In some cases, there may also be enrichment activities that relate the reading to writing, art, drama, or music experiences.

51. C: In lessons about color as one element of visual arts, preschool children can learn the names of different colors (A); skills of sensory discrimination (B) in telling different colors apart from each other; and skills of classification (D) by separating different colors and experimenting with mixing colors to see what other colors they produce.

52. B: For preadolescents and younger adolescents to resolve Erikson's psychosocial nuclear conflict of Industry vs. Inferiority (typically described as from age 7–12, but individual differences can make it earlier or later), they must experience success in school. For students to transition from Piaget's cognitive Concrete Operations to Formal Operations stage (A), teachers can start them with logical reasoning involving concrete manipulatives and then gradually progress, scaffolding as needed, to abstract reasoning without concrete objects. Forming action plans for the future that they find satisfying (C) is an activity that helps older adolescents to resolve Erikson's psychosocial conflict of Identity vs. Role Confusion. Students typically need to transition cognitively from intuitive thought to logical reasoning (D), i.e., from Piaget's Preoperational to Concrete Operations stage, during early childhood, not adolescence.

53. D: This activity best illustrates instruction in the visual art element of line, as the children are working with outlines and experimenting with drawing lines. An activity in color could involve identifying different colors in a work of art and mixing paint colors. An activity in shape might involve identifying different shapes in an artwork and arranging shapes to make pictures. An activity with light could entail identifying light and dark areas of artworks and selecting similar pieces to create contrasts.

54. A: When preschool teachers assign cooperative activities, children can learn to verbalize what they want. They can learn empathy (B) through discussion and question-answer groups. They can learn cooperation through small-group collaborative projects their teachers assign (C), as well as how to take turns (D), listen to others, and express what they want verbally.

55. B: Only choice B is correct. Research shows that more physically active children tend to do better on standardized academic tests. Choices A, C, and D are incorrect because research actually finds that more physical activity improves attention, working memory, and problem-solving, rather than the reverse.

56. C: EC aesthetic learning activities that concentrate on textures are a good way to enhance children's developing skills in representing things symbolically. Contrary to (D), symbolic representation is an ability that typically develops before preschool, most often between the ages of 18 and 24 months. Toddlers begin using toys/objects to represent other objects, and progress after around 2 years old to dramatic pretend/make-believe play, wherein people play roles representing other people. Feeling textures without seeing them (A) is one good way to learn about textures, as when EC teachers give them "feely bags" to learn to describe textures by feel alone. However, teachers should *also* have children examine the textures of things visually and have them explore how to represent textures in visual ways. In addition to the tactile and visual modalities, children's vocabulary *is* enhanced (B) when teachers ask them to supply specific words to describe various textures (e.g., prickly, fuzzy, spongy, cushy, sharp, dull, soft, hard, bumpy, smooth, etc.).

57. C: Helping young children understand that communication can occur in different ways, including both verbally and nonverbally, is an important component of developing their speaking and listening skills. Verbal communication refers to spoken language, volume, and intonation, whereas nonverbal communication includes such elements as eye contact, gestures, physical distance, and body language. Incorporating both forms of communication into the classroom for different purposes helps students learn to listen and respond appropriately in a variety of contexts. Further, this strategy supports students' oral language development, as accompanying verbal communication with nonverbal cues strengthens their understanding of its meaning.

58. A: Young children are naturally inclined to make observations about the world around them as they learn, process, organize, and test new ideas. Creating learning opportunities in which students are encouraged to do so promotes learning and development in science by fostering their inherent sense of curiosity, inquiry, and exploration. By selecting students each week to conduct a daily weather report and recording it on a class weather chart, this teacher prompts students to think scientifically about this concept by asking them to make observations about the natural environment to identify patterns and make predictions.

59. D: To deepen young children's comprehension of word meanings, teachers should provide them with multiple definitions and examples for each word rather than only one (A). They should introduce new concepts together with new vocabulary words (B) associated with the concepts. They should provide additional information to give children's comprehension of meanings more depth (C).

60. A: By asking the child to come up with alternative criteria for sorting (e.g., by size, shape, or weight instead of by color), the teacher is helping the child to develop problem-solving skills in thinking of a variety of alternative solutions/answers. Telling the child that he or she is performing classification (B) is a better example of teaching formal math vocabulary by connecting it with informal math activity rather than promoting problem solving. Asking the child how he or she is sorting the rocks (C) is a better example of promoting math communication through explaining the sorting criterion rather than promoting problem solving.

61. B: The quality of health and nutrition significantly impacts nearly all aspects of learning and development among young children. These factors contribute to students' energy levels, ability to focus and sustain attention in class, working memory, and emotional regulation. Further, adequate health and nutrition are necessary for proper long-term cognitive, physical, social, and emotional development. Teaching young children about the importance of nutrition and maintaining a healthy lifestyle establishes a foundation for encouraging healthy choices throughout life. In addition, teachers must know how to recognize when students' health and nutritional needs are not being met so as to provide the appropriate support and resources.

62. A: According to educational and literacy experts, teachers can sustain young children's interest and enthusiasm for writing by providing them with a variety of different writing activities rather than letting them get bored by always assigning the same kinds of writing tasks. Teachers can also set up "writing corners" in their classrooms including writing contributions from children and teachers that demonstrate a variety of kinds and styles of writing. Adults and children alike enjoy tasks that are fun, so teachers *should* offer these (B) to make writing enjoyable rather than a chore. Experts advise teachers to transcribe what young children dictate, and have children practice sounding out and spelling words as they say them. They also *do* recommend that teachers deliberately make some transcription errors for children to spot and correct (C). Another recommendation is to let young children each take turns contributing one sentence to a daily class newsletter; assigning each child to write an entire one alone (D) is an inappropriate demand for most young children/beginning writers.

63. A: A calendar is one type of chart. We use charts and graphs to organize information, interpret it, and more readily visualize relationships within the information. Using calendars can help young children understand how information is organized by showing them this organization visually in graphic form. Statistical tables showing differences among groups or individuals are commonly used by scientists to present the results of their research studies but are not as appropriate for very young children. Line graphs are better for depicting changes over time. Weather forecasts are better for helping children understand how scientists predict probabilities, i.e., the chances something will happen.

64. A: Piaget demonstrated through experiments with very young children that they cannot yet perform logical or mathematical mental operations like dividing a whole into parts. They focus on only one aspect or property of an object rather than multiple properties; Piaget named this *centration.* When children in Piaget's Preoperational stage see several pieces of an apple, they see the total number of pieces rather than their sizes and assume several pieces equal more than one whole apple. Therefore they do not yet understand the part-whole concept {(B), (D)}, even if they can use concrete objects (C). Children in Piaget's Concrete Operations stage, around elementary school age, can understand these concepts as long as they are accompanied by concrete objects.

They cannot understand them abstractly without concrete examples until Piaget's stage of Formal Operations, around the preteen to teen ages.

65. A: Teaching young children how to repurpose discarded items shows the concept of recycling as a form of waste management. Doing so demonstrates in a developmentally appropriate context how waste is generated, and how individuals can reduce it to protect the environment. Integrating this concept into daily activities, such as art projects, develops students' understanding of how recycling contributes to managing waste, while encouraging their sense of personal responsibility toward caring for the environment.

66. D: An effective way to help young children develop early math skills related to measurement is to ask them to help with everyday chores and activities that incorporate measurement—e.g., shopping, cooking, sewing, gardening, etc.—and use these activities to discuss measurement concepts and processes with the children as they participate directly, which is more effective than if they only watch the adult demonstrate (C). Adults should *not* discourage young children from using their own personal units of measurement (A); this is a natural and useful practice, as when a child says his friend is as tall as four teddy bears. Adults can moreover apply this practice to describe measurements in ways young children can understand better than if they tried to teach them standardized units of measurement in isolated lessons (B) with no real-life referents.

67. B: Receptive and expressive language skills are fundamental to literacy development among young children. Receptive language skills (the ability to understand and internalize language) are necessary for developing expressive language skills (the ability to accurately produce language). Both are necessary for building the background knowledge and vocabulary necessary for effective skill development in all areas of literacy, and therefore must be emphasized in the early childhood classroom. By reading aloud to students and providing explanations and visual examples, the teacher conscientiously promotes receptive language skill development. Further, in asking an open-ended question after the read-aloud, the teacher encourages expressive language skill development by prompting students to use expanded vocabulary to describe their favorite parts of the story.

68. A: Implementing activities to promote students' oral language skills is integral to establishing a foundation for literacy development and academic achievement across content areas. Teaching prekindergarten students to listen responsively enhances a variety of skills, including receptive language, communication, and problem-solving. Incorporating listening games that include simple, multi-step directions provides young children with the opportunity to practice this skill in an engaging and developmentally-appropriate setting. When implementing such activities, teachers must ensure directions are clear, concise, and limited to only a few steps, so as not to distract, confuse, or overwhelm students.

69. B: Among tasks that require and teach phonological awareness, hearing sounds or phonemes within words that rhyme is the easiest of the choices given. Being able to manipulate phonemes by replacing one sound in a word with another sound to make a new word (e.g., changing *cat* to *hat*) is one of the hardest tasks. Being able to isolate or separate sounds in words and to classify them as initial, medial, or final sounds in words is easier than manipulating them but harder than working with rhymes. Blending phonemes and syllables (i.e., combining them into words) and segmenting or separating words into their component syllables and sounds are both easier than manipulating phonemes but harder than isolating and classifying them.

70. B: Morphology is the smallest structural units that determine grammatical differences in meaning, like the *–s* ending differentiating the singular noun *book* from the plural *books*. Phonology (A) is the rules for combining a language's phonemes or speech sounds into syllables and words.

Syntax (C) is the ordering of words and structuring of word combinations to make grammatical sentences. Semantics (D) is the meanings of the words in a language.

71. B: Predictable books are those that feature repetition and structured patterns throughout the text. This is an advantage for young children learning to read because the repetition affords familiarity, allowing children to participate immediately in the story and also to remember and practice words and language patterns. Predictability refers to repetition, not to a lack of plot originality or imagination. They usually contain pictures and do not generally use complex sentences.

72. A: Teachers should keep from confusing young children by introducing letters to them that have similar sounds in separate lessons. They should introduce continuous consonant sounds (f, r, s, m, n), which are easier to produce in isolation with less distortion, before they teach consonant sounds that are stops (p, b, t, d, k, g), which are more difficult for young children to produce, not vice versa (B). Letters with similar appearances should be presented during separate lessons, not the same one (C), also to prevent confusion. Teachers should introduce high-utility letters/sounds first, not low-utility (D), as the high-utility ones are those they will hear, see, and use most often.

73. C: When the teacher lets children choose their favorite colors of stickers, they are getting practice for the future collection of data. When they match their sticker colors to corresponding colors on a piece of poster board, they are getting practice in the future organization of data. And when they see their and the other children's stickers placed on this poster as a chart that everybody can see, they are getting practice for their future display of data they have collected and organized. Identifying sticker shapes (A) is more relevant to learning figure properties. Guessing how many stickers of each color were chosen (B) is more relevant to practice in predicting probabilities. Choosing stickers as rewards for something until they accumulate enough to receive a larger reward (D) is more relevant to a token economy, used in behaviorism to increase the incidence of desired behaviors and decrease undesired ones.

74. A: Understanding the concept of measurement is essential to developing skills across subject areas and in multiple real-world situations. Further, introducing measurement in early childhood establishes the foundation of understanding necessary for students to grasp increasingly complex topics, such as volume, height, weight, and mass. To introduce this idea, teachers should begin with the notion that some objects are larger or smaller than others, which prompts students to recognize differences in size. By asking students to arrange blocks from largest to smallest, this teacher encourages them to notice the size of each block and sort them accordingly, promoting early development of measurement skills.

75. D: Differentiated instruction models to address the needs of diverse students involve varying teacher roles, including highly active and directive one-on-one intensive trainers for students with profound disabilities; part-time instructors of whole classes; part-time tutors of individual students; and occasional advisors and consultants to independent study projects. Traditional teacher-centered instructional models primarily involve active teacher roles, with more passive student roles. Progressive student-centered instructional models primarily involve more active student roles, with less active and directive teacher roles as guides and facilitators. Small-group cooperative learning models involve teacher roles as part-time facilitators and guides.

76. B: Reading comprehension problems can be indicated by either or both: focusing on details to the exclusion of main concepts, i.e., "missing the forest for the trees," (A) can signal inadequate comprehension; but even when understanding the main ideas, being unable to relate any details (C) like a story's setting, characters' appearances, etc., can equally signify comprehension problems.

Good comprehension enables both understanding the main points and also noticing and retaining supporting details. In addition, even if a student gets the main ideas, an inability to retell logical sequences of events in the reading (D) is a sign that the student's reading comprehension is deficient.

77. B: When teachers design integrated ECE curricula organized around themes, they can not only use themes that appeal to young children, but they can also address individual differences among children (A), including individual strengths in various learning modalities. Approaching unit planning thematically offers many natural opportunities to offer hands-on learning activities for young children (B). A thematic approach to the integrated curriculum is also readily adaptable to being evaluated through portfolio assessments and performance-based assessments (C). Thematic organization of curriculum units makes learning more meaningful to young children while still allowing teachers to couch specific benchmarks for learning concepts and skills by age and/or developmental level within themes of interest to children (D).

78. B: In language arts, sequencing refers to one's ability to recall and retell events of a text in the order in which they occurred. Teaching this important skill is essential to promoting success across content areas, as it contributes to the development of reading comprehension and writing, as well as the ability to understand and respond appropriately to directions. By kindergarten, students can reasonably be expected to retell the major events of a fictional work of literature in the order in which they occurred using visual aids as support. In this situation, having students sort events from the story using picture cards would most effectively promote their sequencing abilities.

79. C: Understanding basic concepts of print is a fundamental skill for emergent literacy development in young children. While most prekindergarten students have not yet learned to read fluently, it is still important to demonstrate the prevalence and application of printed language in daily life. This includes teaching young children about the purpose and use of printed books. Modeling how to hold a book, turn pages, read from left to right, and pointing out key characteristics, such as a book's title, cover, and author's name, develops print awareness in prekindergarten students. Doing so promotes students' understanding that books contain printed words that convey meaning, establishing a foundation for emergent literacy development.

80. A: One instructional technique teachers can use to address individual differences among students in the same class—not just for classes with homogeneous student levels (d) (which seldom happens anyway)—is assigning small groups, both for re-teaching skills or concepts to struggling students and for offering enrichment activities to advanced students, not just for one (b) or the other (c).

Professionalism and Collaborative Partnerships

81. D: By law, ECE employees are required to report suspected child abuse or neglect and are also immune from liability for releasing student records related to such reporting. The Family Educational Rights and Privacy Act (FERPA) mandates student records confidentiality for every ECE program, facility, or agency that receives federal funding, not every ECE program, facility, or agency in the country. IDEA (Individuals with Disabilities Education Act) is a federal law and hence not superseded by state special education laws.

82. D: EC educators interact positively when they use problem-solving activities and dialogues to help them discover which learning experiences they can make more effective for children, and how to do this. Sharing anecdotal records and observations with other educators within the ECE program for the purpose of improving instruction does not disrespect privacy (A). Communicating with other adults within the ECE setting about the children and families they serve does not violate confidentiality (B) but does constitute positive interaction. EC educators within a program should not only share their observations and records of their students, but should moreover use this shared information to collaboratively plan their instruction (C).

83. C: The law stipulates that EC teachers and other professionals working with children and families are "mandated reporters" who are legally required to report any suspicions of child abuse or neglect. The teacher should report her suspicions to authorities because this law was enacted to stop violence against children, and not just because the law incurs penalties against professionals who do not comply with it (D). Even if the teacher feels sorry for the mother, and/or she cannot prove her suspicions, these are not reasons to refrain from reporting them (A). She should report seeing injuries to the child and hearing from the child that the boyfriend caused them, even though she knows the mother depends financially and emotionally on the boyfriend (B). Avoiding potentially harmful side effects for the mother is no justification for allowing suspected abuse to go unreported.

84. B: Frequent communication with students' families is integral to establishing positive, collaborative relationships between the school and home that enhance the overall learning experience. Students come from a variety of backgrounds, living situations, and family dynamics, so the teacher must consider and accommodate the communication needs of all families. Using multiple methods of communication ensures accessibility and inclusivity for all students' families, promoting the positive relationships necessary for student development and learning.

85. D: Under the Family Educational Rights and Privacy Act (FERPA), teachers may only disclose students' educational records—including personally identifiable information—to the student's legal caregivers or in specific authorized situations. Although classroom photos may be posted online, teachers must adhere to the guidelines of FERPA when doing so. Photographs may not reveal any personally identifiable information related to students, such as names, birthdates, or identification numbers, and may not focus on an individual student. Teachers must also follow the protocols outlined by the school district regarding posting classroom photographs online.

86. C: Effective conferences rely on positive and productive communication between the school staff and students' families. To achieve this, it is important that the teacher establishes a welcoming atmosphere in which family members feel included as active participants in their child's learning. This includes beginning a conference with positive remarks about the student, asking relevant questions, and actively listening and responding to the family's concerns. Then, students' families will likely feel more inclined to share important information about their child, such as learning styles, individual needs, and interests that would allow the teacher to design more effective and engaging instruction.

87. C: One way early childhood educators can include families in children's education is to acknowledge the integral part that parents play in supporting their children's learning. Another way is for educators to promote and support parenting skills, their enhancement, and their application by parents. To include families, educators should work to achieve reciprocal and regular communication between the school and family. All school personnel should not only make parents feel welcome at the school; they should also seek out help and support from parents.

88. B: Professional communication is one of the areas of teacher performance typically evaluated in performance appraisal systems, as is the teacher's professional development; teacher compliance with policies and procedures, including procedures for operation and other requirements; and improvement in academic performance for all students, not only identified ones.

89. C: Educators support students in succeeding academically by encouraging parents to participate actively. For example, they can help parents converse in ways that prepare their children for classroom communications. Engaging parents promotes mutual understanding of parent, classroom, and school expectations of teachers and students, supporting student success. Helping immigrant/undereducated parents pursue ESL and GED programs allows parents to better support their children academically. Educators can also involve and help parents by referring them to community resources with arts, sports, and science programs, homework help, etc.

90. D: A number of US states issue teacher certification/licensure to bachelor's-degree graduates for one or two years but expect them to gain master's degrees (or other additional certification) in the interim. Teachers earn more advanced licensure when they meet goals established by their US states. Even teachers with advanced graduate degrees must continue setting and meeting goals throughout their careers. In addition to adding credentials, taking courses, and attending workshops, seminars, and conferences, reading professional literature can be a PD goal.

91. D: Teacher appraisals and evaluations are mostly regulated at state and local levels. While federal regulations did heavily control appraisals in the past, since the passing of the Every Student Succeeds Act, power over teacher appraisals largely rests with the state.

92. D: One teacher PD route is professional organizations' courses, workshops, and conferences, though this is not the only way (a). Although teachers must stay at school slightly longer than students, and many stay even later to complete work, school days still end earlier than other workdays; and unlike other professionals, teachers get summers off, so working teachers often take graduate courses (b), both individually and as part of advanced degree programs—not only in their original subjects (c), but often in additional subjects/specialties (d), e.g., adding science to math, ESL to English, special to regular education, etc.

93. B: Researchers have found that Hispanic families in the US are more likely to choose home- and family-based child care and preschool education than outside centers. This may reflect the collectivist nature of Latin culture, which values social interactions and relationships more than structure. Caucasian parents in the US are found to prefer preschool centers. This reflects not only the North American culture's individualistic emphasis on structured early learning, and predominant North American custom, but also North American Caucasian parents' attention to scientific findings that center-based preschool education improves children's school readiness skills.

94. B: Administrators of ECE facilities must designate vehicles to use and employees responsible for transportation if an emergency cannot safely wait for the child's parents to arrive but does not require an ambulance. However, when an emergency is non-life-threatening, staff should ask parents when available to transport their children (A). Administrators should keep the number of staff involved in emergency medical treatment to a minimum (C). The staff members designated by administrators to assist in medical emergencies should have current first aid training (D) and be willing to take the responsibility.

95. B: Very little research in the early childhood education field addresses how collaboration among adults influences the children they teach; however, there are some early childhood education curriculum models and approaches that do address interactions among adults (e.g., the High Scope curriculum, the Creative Curriculum, etc.), primarily by pointing out that planning instruction and sharing responsibilities and information rely on teamwork among educators. Unlike early childhood education curriculum models but like early childhood education research literature, professional development and training programs in the field rarely cover or teach adult conflict resolution, how to work collaboratively, or adult learning principles. Thus, early childhood educators must consciously apply teamwork, collaborative planning, and sharing of instructional goals and information toward supporting children's positive development.

96. D: When EC teachers send home letters to parents at the beginning of the school year, the parents perceive the teachers as more available and approachable. When an EC teacher calls each parent during the first two weeks of the school year, parents are more likely to appreciate and enjoy these conversations than to feel alarmed (A) by them. Calling parents early in the year also makes it easier to call them again later in the year if child issues warrant it (B). When EC teachers publish a weekly or monthly class newsletter online, through e-mail, or in print, parents learn to expect communication from them (C).

97. A: An important element of school-community partnerships is outreach by schools to solicit the involvement and support of community members. Another is that schools should offer community members varied, not standard, means of school involvement (B). Another is that schools should emphasize two-way, not unilateral, communication (C) with their communities. Another is that schools should work to redefine perceptions of schools as community learning centers (D).

98. A: If a child at an ECE facility develops a non-emergency illness, the staff must contact the parents. Shared decision making should occur within the bounds of established policies to determine if the child should leave the facility. Non-emergency medical treatments require ECE facilities to file procedures and reports the same as emergency treatments do (B). Parental consent forms should authorize doctors or nurses to provide routine medical treatment (C) of children who are in ECE facilities. Information on children's chronic medical conditions and directions for their treatment should not only be on file in ECE facilities, but should also always be posted for staff access (D).

99. C: Both culturally diverse families and American educators experience equal problems in their interactions. Educators and diverse families both have difficulties dealing with foreign languages, different customs and behaviors, and major differences in the educational systems with which they are familiar—including different laws for special education. Thus, neither the families (A) nor the educators (B) experience greater difficulty than the other. Moreover, the challenges both groups experience are not necessarily or even usually very minimal (D) in nature; they can be quite substantial.

100. A: The Education Practices Commission can revoke an educator's certificate for pursuing and/or obtaining certification using fraudulent means; *knowingly* (not unwittingly) failing to report suspected child abuse (b); *proven* (not suspected) incompetence for teaching or other duties in a school (c); and both pleading guilty to and being convicted of a crime (d) or criminal charge (including felonies, misdemeanors, or anything other than minor traffic violations).

Practice Test #2

Early Childhood Development and Learning

1. Which of these is generally accepted as indicating possible delayed or atypical intellectual development in a child?

a. A standardized IQ test score that is 10 points lower than the mean
b. A standardized IQ test score one standard deviation below the mean
c. A standardized IQ test score two standard deviations below the mean
d. A standardized IQ test score is never used for indicating this possibility

2. Of the following, which is most accurate about the timing of children's speech development?

a. Children speaking fewer than 50 words by 18–24 months will always be needing therapy.
b. Children speaking fewer than 50 words by 18–24 months may or may not need therapy.
c. Children speaking fewer than 50 words by 18–24 months are normal, needing no therapy.
d. Children speaking fewer than 50 words by 18–24 months in baby talk must have therapy.

3. A student taking a test answers one question correctly but fails to answer a different question that was meant to test the same construct. This test is most likely lacking which kind of reliability?

a. Internal consistency reliability
b. Parallel forms reliability
c. Test-retest reliability
d. Inter-rater reliability

4. For teachers to make informal assessments of pre-K classes, which of these would apply?

a. Teachers assess during small-group rather than whole-class activities.
b. Teachers only make assessments during activities for the whole class.
c. Teachers can organize assessments by using around 10 themes a day.
d. Teachers make classroom observations each targeting different skills.

5. Which of these is correct regarding expert guidelines for indoor and outdoor spaces in EC learning environments?

a. Children's products and other visual elements should be put at adult eye level.
b. Spaces should be arranged for individual, small-group, and large-group activity.
c. Spaces should be organized to prohibit children from moving among activities.
d. Spaces should be arranged so children are not distracted by social interactions.

6. What is correct regarding predictive validity, sensitivity, specificity, and false-positive and false-negative errors in screening and assessment instruments used with preschool children?

a. A screening tool identifies a potential mental health disorder which a complete evaluation then diagnoses.
b. An instrument correctly identifying 6 of 10 children with disorders/delays is said to have a specificity of 60%.
c. An instrument correctly identifying 8 of 10 children as not having disorders/delays shows sensitivity of 80%.
d. A screening tool identifying delays or disorders in children where none exists contains false-negative errors.

7. Which of the following reflects application of Freud's third stage of development to early childhood practices?

a. Not taking personally when a 4-year-old rejects the same-sex parent for the other-sex parent
b. Being careful during toilet-training of toddlers not to focus excessive attention on the process
c. Making sure that any objects that baby can reach and mouth are not dangerous or unsanitary
d. Not taking personally when 7-year-olds shift their attention from their parents to their friends

8. How are instructional objectives that apply Bloom's Taxonomy also influenced by a major principle of behaviorist learning theory?

a. They use Bloom's Taxonomy terms requiring students to remember and understand.
b. They use only action verbs to describe how students must demonstrate their learning.
c. They use only behaviorist methods of changing behavior for teaching new information.
d. They use only behaviors that can be externally observed, whether measurable or not.

9. Adult interviews used to gather screening/assessment information about infants and young children:

a. Are conducted in structured formats with assigned questions.
b. Are in semi-structured formats using administrator judgment.
c. Cover only the child's identified areas of strengths and needs.
d. Are brief but usually still longer than self-reporting measures.

10. Which of the following did Piaget say children develop at the oldest ages?

a. Magical thinking
b. Symbolic thinking
c. Intuitive thinking
d. Deductive logic

11. Of the following, which is correct about considerations in arranging indoor learning environments to fit with curriculum planning for toddlers and preschoolers?

a. Rooms should be arranged to limit activities to certain areas.
b. The floors in all the rooms should be covered with carpeting.
c. The rooms should be organized to enable different activities.
d. Math and science activities should be in one classroom area.

12. How can assessment results be applied to instructional planning for ECE groups and individual children?

a. If EC educators record careful anecdotal observations and authentic assessments, outlines are not necessary.
b. Making organized outlines of developmental guidelines gives bases for anecdotal and authentic assessments.
c. The extensive practice and review needed for young children to retain skills are outside of ECE program scope.
d. Developmental sequences are irrelevant to systems that ECE programs utilize for tracking children's progress.

13. Which of these is a benefit students receive from continuous student performance monitoring and charting?

a. Students receive visual illustrations of what they learn.
b. Students receive delayed feedback from the teachers.
c. Students receive graphs and goals only from a teacher.
d. Students receive practice through independent study.

14. What is accurate about different screening and assessment instruments used in EC education programs?

a. All these instruments measure the same developmental domains.
b. These instruments are all meant for use with the same applications.
c. Not all of these are appropriate with ethnically diverse populations.
d. The same methods of administration are used with all instruments.

15. Among the following, which statement applies most to applying assessment results in planning ECE instruction?

a. Lesson plans should promote developmental guidelines rather than child interests.
b. Tracking progress should be systematic, but need not follow developmental order.
c. Organizing outlines of developmentally appropriate guidelines informs assessment.
d. Added support should be enriched for children below class level, and 1:1 for above.

16. Of the following, which is more typical of a screening instrument than an assessment instrument?

a. Interpreting scores by weighting various item values
b. Interpreting scores by reversing point values of items
c. Interpreting scores by comparisons to national norms
d. Interpreting scores by comparisons to a cut-off score

17. At what age should a typically developing child be able to tell others his/her name, age, and sex?

a. Two years
b. Four years
c. One year
d. Three years

18. Which of these is accurate concerning formal assessment instruments used in early childhood education?

a. Formal assessment instruments cannot prevent administrator bias.
b. Formal assessment instruments record more than child responses.
c. Formal assessment data should not be compared by ages or levels.
d. Formal assessments are typically standardized tests given to groups.

19. What is most accurate regarding formal and informal observations for the screening and assessment of EC populations?

a. Informal observations are less likely to need training for administration.
b. Formal observations are made of children's activities in natural settings.
c. Informal observations are conducted of children in structured activities.
d. Formal observations usually take less time than informal observations.

20. Which of the following characteristics in children's language development typically occurs latest?

a. Responding to requests ("Give it to Mom") and questions ("More juice?")
b. Wanting to hear the same stories, games, or rhymes repeated many times
c. Answering simple questions about stories they enjoy hearing read or told
d. Being able to point at a few of their body parts when someone asks them

21. In which of Brown's Stages of Syntactical and Morphological Development would a child be if s/he uses constructions such as, "They're coming" and "She's here"?

a. Stage III
b. Stage IV
c. Stage V
d. Stage II

22. Which of these reflects valid applications of screening and/or assessment instruments in ECE programs?

a. Evaluating children's achievement of program goal-related learning outcomes is an inappropriate use.
b. Children's progress and changes over time should be monitored using other tools than assessments.
c. Teacher effectiveness for furthering children's achievement of learning outcomes can be evaluated.
d. EC educators never apply the results of assessments in planning curriculum or treatment programs.

23. During which age range do children's motor skills normally develop the fastest?

a. Infancy (0-2 years)
b. Early childhood (2-6 years)
c. Middle childhood (6-9 years)
d. Late childhood (9-12 years)

24. Which of these most accurately reflects expert recommendations of effective strategies for resolving classroom conflicts?

a. De-emphasize conflicts by not letting students record them.
b. Have students record observations, identifying participants.
c. Discuss student reactions without judging them good or bad.
d. Have students track conflicts over time and discuss reactions.

25. Which of the following is a correct definition of functional behavior analysis?

a. Analyzing whether a behavior is functional or not
b. Analyzing what function is served by the behavior
c. Analyzing to what degree a behavior is functional
d. Making an analysis that is functional of behaviors

26. Children can typically understand and follow simple directions, especially with physical and/or vocal cues, by which of these ages?

a. 6 months
b. 8 months
c. 12 months
d. 18 months

27. In Lawrence Kohlberg's theory of moral development, which two stages are included in his Level 1 of Preconventional Morality?

a. Obedience and Punishment, Individualism and Exchange
b. Individualism and Exchange, Interpersonal Relationships
c. Maintaining Social Order, Social Contract and Individual Rights
d. Social Contract and Individual Rights, Universal Ethical Principles

28. What is true about general behavior management principles for early childhood?

a. Adults need to make rules, but they do not always need to follow them.
b. Adults need only repeat rules that they made a few times for young children.
c. Adults must always consistently enforce whichever rules they establish.
d. Adults should only reward children for good behaviors some of the time.

29. Based on research findings, how does role-playing contribute to effective conflict resolution in the classroom?

a. Role-playing makes conflicts appear less humorous.
b. Role-playing focuses students on their own feelings.
c. Role-playing teaches perspective-taking and empathy.
d. Role-playing promotes subjective reactions to conflict.

30. Which of the following correctly reflects the hierarchy of Bloom's Taxonomy in its most recent (2001) revision?

a. Understanding information comes before remembering it.
b. The analysis of information comes before its application.
c. The organization is by types, not by levels of difficulty.
d. Evaluation of information comes before its creation.

31. As one of the first psychological theorists to study birth order in personality development, Alfred Adler found which of these most important to development?

a. A child's ordinal position of birth
b. The child's psychological position
c. He found both equally important.
d. He found no effects of either one.

32. Of the following, which choice correctly sequences the levels of Bloom's Taxonomy from the simplest cognitive tasks to the most challenging ones?

a. Analyzing, Understanding, Remembering, Creating, Evaluating, Applying
b. Understanding, Remembering, Analyzing, Applying, Creating, Evaluating
c. Analyzing, Remembering, Applying, Creating, Evaluating, Understanding
d. Remembering, Understanding, Applying, Analyzing, Evaluating, Creating

33. According to Erikson, which stage of social behavior is most typical of children around 2–3 years old?

a. Developing control over their physical skills
b. Developing control over their environment
c. Developing trust in parents' meeting needs
d. Developing friendships and success at tasks

34. A kindergarten class activity involves building shapes using a variety of materials. As students work, the teacher conducts observations using a checklist to determine their mastery of the concept. This strategy is an example of which of the following?

a. Diagnostic assessment
b. Summative assessment
c. Formative assessment
d. Authentic assessment

35. Which of these is accurate about how temperament can influence behavior in young children?

a. Children with "easy" temperaments are more likely to give up when first attempts do not succeed.
b. Children with "difficult" temperaments are more likely to be persistent and to welcome challenges.
c. Children with "easy" temperaments are more likely to make repeated trials and handle frustration.
d. Children with "slow to warm up" temperaments will not persist at tasks despite being encouraged.

36. According to Jean Piaget's theory of cognitive development in children, prekindergarten students are most likely to engage in:

a. Circular reactions
b. Logical problem-solving
c. Symbolic play
d. Abstract reasoning

37. Which of the following is generally the most difficult phonemic awareness task for young children?

a. Recognizing rhyming words
b. Blending phonemes
c. Manipulating phonemes
d. Categorizing phonemes

38. A kindergarten teacher has noticed that one student tends to avoid eye contact when speaking, engages in repetitive hand gestures, and becomes agitated by loud noises in the classroom. The student also struggles with various grade-level-appropriate skills, such as grasping writing utensils, using scissors, and zipping a coat. These characteristics may be indicative of which of the following?

a. A learning disability that impacts the development of self-help skills
b. Potential neglect at home
c. A linguistic developmental delay
d. A developmental disorder that affects progression across domains

39. In indoor EC learning environments, which of the following is most related to providing for children's privacy needs?

a. Adult laps for cuddling
b. Pillows and soft upholstery
c. Areas of floor with thick carpets
d. Small inner rooms and partitions

40. A child who correctly uses irregular past tenses of verbs, e.g. *went, fell, froze,* etc., would be in which of Roger Brown's Stages of Syntactic and Morphological Development?

a. Stage I
b. Stage II
c. Stage III
d. Stage IV

Content Knowledge and Responsive Teaching Strategies

41. Which of the following should adults include in their conversations with young children to help them build strong oral language skills?

a. Simple vocabulary and simple sentence structures
b. Primarily telling things rather than asking questions
c. Doing the majority of the talking to model for them
d. Questions requiring them to express abstract ideas

42. What statement is correct regarding motor development activities for preschoolers?

a. Tying shoes, stringing beads, and drawing develop gross-motor skills.
b. Incorporating fine-motor activities into playtime is effective.
c. Running, kicking, throwing, and catching all develop fine-motor skills.
d. Games with rules are better for children than unstructured exercise.

43. Which of the following is an example of experiential learning?

a. Watching a video, taking notes
b. Reading a textbook, taking notes
c. Testing a hypothesis, taking notes
d. Listening to a lecture, taking notes

44. Which of the following would likely be the LEAST effective technique for early childhood teachers to promote oral language and vocabulary development using shared reading?

a. Pointing to book illustrations of new words
b. Relating new words to words children know
c. Giving many varied examples of new words
d. Having children read on their own without teacher intervention

45. Which of the following is NOT true about the whole language approach to literacy instruction?

a. The whole language approach is effective for children with language processing disorders.
b. The whole language approach is effective for supporting constructivist learning of literacy.
c. The whole language approach is effective for integrating literacy across content domains.
d. The whole language approach is effective for emphasizing cultural diversity in instruction.

46. National standards for mathematics instruction dictate that children from preschool through second grade should be able to do which of these relative to data-based inferences and predictions?

a. Be able to talk about events as "likely" or "unlikely" based on their experiences
b. Be able to propose predictions and justify them based on data that they gather
c. Be able to collect and analyze data, draw conclusions, and justify them with data
d. Be able to make inferences/predictions and design studies to investigate these

47. What is a correct conclusion showing internal consistency in instruments used to test preschoolers?

a. Different questions, tasks, and stimuli within one instrument all measure aspects of the same construct.
b. In a comprehensive test of multiple developmental domains, all of the subscale scores should correlate.
c. In a comprehensive test of multiple domains, the scores for subscales correlate with the full-scale score.
d. Children with different developmental needs make similar scores from different items on the same test.

48. A teacher wants to create activities that cover abstract concepts and relationships through the physical handling, exploring, and manipulating of solid objects with different textures. Which kind of activity is represented here?

a. Visual
b. Kinesthetic
c. Auditory
d. Concrete

49. When should teachers write lesson plans for effective organization and implementation?

a. After creating the plan of study but before the lesson plan calendar
b. After a plan of study, units, timelines, and lesson plan calendar
c. After planning instructional unit but before planning timelines
d. After making a lesson plan calendar but before planning the units

50. Which of the following principles of physical growth also applies to motor skills development?

a. Both cephalocaudal and proximodistal
b. Cephalocaudal
c. Proximodistal
d. Neither cephalocaudal nor proximodistal

51. When preschool teachers engage children in activities such as portraying various emotions through physical postures and movements, which is most accurate about the learning outcomes?

a. The movements provide negligible exercise.
b. Children learn ways of expressing emotions.
c. Children understand feelings but have no fun.
d. Children have fun but do not think creatively.

52. Interactive learning activities can overlap with which other instructional methods?

a. Indirect instruction activities
b. Independent study activities
c. Experiential learning activities
d. With any, for certain activities

53. Of the following statements, which is true of how children's mathematical counting skills develop?

a. Learning to count from one to twelve involves more unusual rules.
b. Learning to count from thirteen to nineteen requires more memorizing.
c. Learning to count above twenty involves less consistent rules.
d. Learning to count from twenty to one hundred, children discover base ten.

54. In linguistic development, which of these are younger children more likely to say than older children?

a. Upon hearing "dog," respond with "cat"; when prompted "eat," respond with "drink"
b. Upon hearing "dog," respond with "barks"; upon hearing "eat," respond with "lunch"
c. Upon hearing "dog," respond with "cat"; when prompted "eat," respond with "lunch"
d. Upon hearing "dog," respond with "barks"; upon hearing "eat," respond with "drink"

55. According to EC experts, which of these is most accurate regarding supporting young children's physical fitness?

a. Adults should choose when and what to do, as young children typically cannot.
b. Adults should primarily give verbal directions to promote language growth.
c. Activities should permit every child's success, irrespective of skill level.
d. Young children need to do a single familiar activity until they master it.

56. Among research-based strategies to enhance student motivation, what is applicable?

a. Students will be overwhelmed by being given too many examples.
b. Students must be taught underlying principles directly by teachers.
c. Students often want to know how content is relevant to their lives.
d. Students succeed in cooperative learning groups without pressure.

57. At the beginning of each school day, a kindergarten teacher reviews the monthly calendar with students. The teacher labels days of the week as "yesterday," "today," and "tomorrow," and asks students to identify important events throughout the month. This strategy is beneficial in developing students' sense of which foundational concept related to social studies?

a. How to differentiate between fact and opinion about important events
b. Personal responsibility when working with a group
c. Time, continuity, and change
d. The importance of structure and routine to the function of an organization

58. In a prekindergarten classroom, students are creating bird feeders using recycled materials and seeds. The teacher plans to hang the feeders outside and allow students to observe as birds come to eat the seeds. This activity is likely intended to introduce which of the following scientific concepts?

a. The life cycle of animals
b. The difference between living and nonliving things
c. The basic needs of animals
d. The fact that animals grow and change over time

59. Which of these is correct regarding teacher assessment of early childhood print awareness using a storybook?

a. Teachers should ask children to point out uppercase/lowercase letters and punctuation marks.
b. It is generally not possible to conduct any accurate assessment of print awareness using a storybook.
c. It is unnecessary to ask children to identify the front, back, spine, and title of the storybook.
d. Children who demonstrate print awareness while reading a storybook are usually ready to move on to reading simple novels independently.

60. A kindergarten teacher is planning a unit on changes that can occur in matter. During one of the lessons, the teacher plans to demonstrate that water takes the shape of its container by having students work in groups to observe what happens when water is transferred between a cup, bowl, and tray. This unit and lesson activity support development of students' understanding of which unifying concept related to scientific learning?

a. Constancy and change
b. Form and function
c. Systems and order
d. Measurement and equilibrium

61. When reading aloud to students, a kindergarten teacher makes sure to speak expressively by pausing at the end of each sentence, changing intonation, and correlating inflection with differences in punctuation within the text. In doing so, the teacher models which of the following?

a. The correct usage of academic language
b. Differences in writing styles of literary and informational texts
c. Interest and enthusiasm for reading
d. The relationship between English grammatical conventions in written and spoken language

62. What statement is most appropriate regarding how teachers can help preschoolers learn to use scientific inquiry and discovery?

a. Children learn best from age-appropriate science textbooks.
b. Teachers can find materials in their everyday environments.
c. Found objects from the natural world are not good materials.
d. Teachers should not obtain materials from local businesses.

63. When characterizing young children, what did Vygotsky mean by the term "private speech" that he coined?

a. Speaking in private dialogue with another child
b. Speaking in private conversations with an adult
c. Speaking silently to themselves in their minds
d. Speaking aloud to themselves during activities

64. EC teachers can use puppet shows to help preschoolers develop their social skills through an entertaining medium. What is true about puppet show content and guiding children's discussion of it?

a. Teachers should not encourage being judgmental by asking if puppets are good or bad.
b. It would be irrelevant to ask children which puppets they liked and which they disliked.
c. This is a good way to demonstrate it is preferable to use words over aggressive action.
d. Children should be allowed to say what occurred but not predict what may occur next or offer alternative behaviors.

65. During a writing activity, a kindergarten teacher prompts students to spell unfamiliar words phonetically. This practice encourages students to use which of the following?

a. Orthographic processing skills
b. Inventive spelling
c. Pre-communicative spelling
d. Decoding skills

66. What are some instructional practices that apply research data showing their effectiveness for augmenting student achievement?

a. Teachers give students global recognition rather than praising specific achievements.
b. Teachers use multimodal instruction to combine linguistic and non-linguistic systems.
c. Teachers can increase student achievement more by classwork than with homework.
d. Teachers aid critical thinking but not achievement via hypothesis forming and testing.

67. A kindergarten teacher is planning to introduce students to word families. A beneficial concept to teach first would be:

a. Automaticity
b. Semantics analysis
c. Onset and rime
d. Prosody

68. A kindergarten teacher wants to begin developing students' ability to think algebraically throughout a unit on adding numbers up to ten. Which of the following strategies would be most effective in achieving this goal?

a. Providing both verbal and written directions on how to add numbers up to ten
b. Modeling how to finger count when adding two numbers
c. Introducing expressions concretely, pictorially, then abstractly
d. Demonstrating where the concept of addition is applicable in real-world situations

69. A group of prekindergarten students is learning about patterns by arranging beads on a string after watching a demonstration from the teacher. Which of the following teacher questions would best promote inquiry and logical reasoning skills as students work?

a. "What color beads are you using?"
b. "Why did you choose this bead to go next in your pattern?"
c. "What kind of pattern are you making with your beads?"
d. "Which bead comes next in your pattern?"

70. A kindergarten teacher is planning a thematic unit on the features of space. Throughout the unit, students will participate in activities such as reading various texts about space and space travel, listening to songs to learn the names of planets, and creating models of the moon, stars, sun, and planets using clay. Which of the following best describes how this instructional approach supports students' learning about objects in the solar system and universe?

a. Integrating scientific instruction across content areas
b. Providing multiple hands-on active learning experiences
c. Using structured and unstructured play opportunities to strengthen learning
d. Providing varied opportunities for students to demonstrate understanding

71. In children's literature, how are picture books typically classified?

a. A genre
b. Both a genre and a format
c. A format
d. Neither genre nor format

72. Which of the following foundational science skills is best illustrated by an activity comparing non-standard measures, such as using scales to find the weight ratio when comparing apples and grapes?

a. Observation
b. Inference
c. Communication
d. Classifying

73. In the art center of a kindergarten classroom, the teacher has included multiple tools of varying sizes, such as pencils, paintbrushes, and crayons. This strategy is likely intended to promote students' development of which of the following?

a. Gross motor skills
b. Artistic expression
c. Fine motor skills
d. Locomotor skills

74. A kindergarten teacher is planning a unit on the characteristics of living and nonliving things in nature. Which of the following activities would be most developmentally appropriate in introducing this concept?

a. Leading a class nature walk focused on identifying living and nonliving things
b. Bringing in samples of living and nonliving things for students to observe
c. Creating a class art project using items from nature
d. Asking open-ended questions about the differences between living and nonliving things in a class discussion

75. Which of the following is NOT correct regarding patterns and relationships relative to early math development?

a. Children need deliberate instruction before they begin to recognize patterns.
b. Children with strong pattern understanding often have strong executive function skills.
c. Awareness and understanding of patterns and relationships support understanding of categorization and rhythm.
d. Awareness and understanding of patterns and relationships aid understanding of art and music as well as math.

76. In which of the following stages of spelling development do children use letters to represent speech sounds in a systematic and understandable way?

a. Correct
b. Transitional
c. Semiphonetic
d. Phonetic

77. What is most accurate about developmentally appropriate motor skill activities for preschoolers?

a. It is more effective to separate playtime from quiet activities.
b. It is more effective to integrate fine-motor activities into play.
c. It is more effective to offer them structured games with rules.
d. It is more effective to plan motor activities with longer times.

78. A kindergarten teacher uses a digital app to provide families with daily updates on students' progress, the curriculum, and important classroom information. Students' families can also use the app to message the teacher individually with questions and concerns regarding their children's performance. Which of the following best describes the benefit of using this resource for communication?

a. Establishing and maintaining partnerships with families to enhance student learning and development
b. Documenting interactions with students' families
c. Improving students' behavior in the classroom
d. Encouraging students' families to become active participants in the education program

79. A kindergarten teacher shows students a jar of red, green, and blue beads. The teacher asks students to predict which color of bead is most prevalent in the jar, and records their responses on a bar graph. Which of the following developmental concepts is this strategy likely intended to support?

a. Estimation and measurement
b. Operations and algebraic thinking
c. Number sense and ordering
d. Data analysis and probability

80. Of these statements, what is most correct about teaching citizenship to young children?

a. EC teachers should use factual material rather than fictional children's literature.
b. Young children are cognitively unable to relate narratives to citizenship concepts.
c. Discussions of rules are best begun with reading real rules rather than narratives.
d. Small-group activities having children write and then revise class rules are useful.

Professionalism and Collaborative Partnerships

81. What is true about guidelines for ECE personnel regarding medications administered to children in EC care and education settings?

a. ECE centers/programs should write their own policies and procedures, regardless of state licensing requirements.
b. ECE experts find it unnecessary for centers to require doctor and parent permission for giving medication to children.
c. If written parent consent to give medication is kept on file, separate charts for staff are redundant and enable errors.
d. Staff should label all medications by drug name, child name, doctor name and contact information, and instructions.

82. Which of these accurately represents child custody issues affecting ECE facilities and types of custody?

a. Legal custody is an individual/agency's right and responsibility to give a child immediate care and housing.
b. One issue that affects ECE facilities is when state authorities have removed a child from parental custody.
c. Two parents pursuing custody of a child but not living together will not have any impact on ECE facilities.
d. Physical custody is an individual/agency's right to decide for a child on housing, education, and medicine.

83. The primary purpose of Title I, Part A of the Elementary and Secondary Education Act is to:

a. Provide academic support to students with learning disabilities.
b. Provide additional support to students from low-income families.
c. Fund the development of parent education programs.
d. Establish partnerships between schools and families.

84. To develop culturally competent teaching practices, teachers must first:

a. Address the various communication needs of students' families
b. Recognize and eliminate their own biases and assumptions toward other cultures
c. Work with colleagues in developing instructional strategies to accommodate diverse learning needs
d. Incorporate elements of students' culture into instruction

85. Which of the following best represents the ultimate goal of the federally funded program, Head Start?

a. Improve student achievement on standardized assessments
b. Provide low-income families with child care
c. Promote the learning and development of prekindergarten students from socioeconomically disadvantaged backgrounds
d. Provide universal access to preschool

86. Which choice reflects expert advice to teachers on communicating with parents?

a. Communicating expectations undermines parent expectations.
b. Focus communications with parents to be about their children.
c. Select one communication method and use it with all parents.
d. Measure communication results and adjust plans accordingly.

87. School districts' professional development committees (PDCs) help educators pursue PD by doing which of the following?

a. PDCs work with new teachers and their mentors but never pay workshop tuition.
b. PDCs ensure PD goals meet district guidelines and document PD for state boards.
c. PDCs work apart from district administrators by setting only interdisciplinary goals.
d. PDCs defer to district administrators for setting district professional teacher goals.

88. Experts report which of the following about reflective teachers relative to appraisals?

a. Reflective teachers excel at self-evaluation but resist others' evaluations.
b. Reflective teachers do not fear evaluations but are unlikely to self-assess.
c. Reflective teachers want self-improvement informed by other educators.
d. Reflective teachers are motivated to improve mainly for better appraisals.

89. Which of the following is true about participation in committees, projects, and other school functions?

a. Participation provides more chances to pursue professional development.
b. Participation in these is generally not worth the time due to a lack of relation to in-class work.
c. These functions focus on information that spans across a wide range of domains instead of focusing on individual content subjects.
d. Participation in sporting events is generally required.

90. Among these forms of educator professional development (PD), which kind enables collaborations on presentations and workshops and promotes information sharing?

a. Mentors
b. Study groups
c. Learning communities
d. Pre-service internships

91. Which of the following professional organizations is a labor union?

a. National Education Association
b. National Association for the Education of Young Children
c. Association for Supervision and Curriculum Development
d. National Council of Teachers of English

92. Which of the following is true regarding how teachers can participate in school or district projects, committees, and other activities?

a. Teachers can only participate in faculty, department, staff, and PTA/PTO meetings.
b. Teachers' participation is only beneficial to students and other teachers.
c. Teachers are unqualified to join committees concerned with the admission of special populations.
d. Teachers can find and choose texts for educational use and contribute to curriculum design.

93. Among areas wherein appraisal systems evaluate teacher performance, what is or is not included?

a. Effective instruction, teacher-centered or student-centered regardless
b. Whether students participate actively and successfully in their learning
c. Evaluation of student progress is more important than giving feedback
d. Discipline is not evaluated like time, materials, and teaching strategies

94. In an elementary school lacking sufficient classroom and office space, a teacher's aide had to sit in the hallway with ELL students to teach them, and a speech-language pathologist had to do therapy with students in the narrow spaces between bookshelves in the library's storage room. Which statement related to these examples is most accurate regarding school factors?

a. Distracting, uncomfortable, and noisy environments impede teaching and learning.
b. Educational environments are not as important as serious issues like riots in school.
c. Even in less than ideal environments, students will learn given sufficient motivation.
d. School factors do not affect teaching and learning as much as community and home.

95. If parents do not pick up children from an ECE center on time, what is true of the ECE center's legal responsibilities?

a. ECE staff are more likely to incur legal liability keeping a child at the center.
b. ECE staff are not likely to incur legal liability taking a child home with them.
c. ECE staff must discuss reasons and solutions with chronically tardy parents.
d. ECE staff should not tell the police if they must remove a child who was left.

96. Which of these is true about what teachers can do using technology?

a. Teachers can communicate with parents using varied methods.
b. Teachers can find all of the texts they use in class for free online.
c. Teachers can read and grade papers but cannot add comments.
d. Teachers can use technology to make instruction largely unnecessary.

97. In the Association of American Educators (AAE) Code of Ethics for Educators, distinguishing school policies from personal opinions is under which principle?

a. Ethical Conduct toward Students
b. Ethical Conduct toward Professional Colleagues
c. Ethical Conduct toward Parents and Community
d. Ethical Conduct toward Practices and Performance

98. What is recommended for ECE facilities to do regarding existing custody arrangements of the children they serve?

a. ECE program administrators can make decisions regarding the legal and physical custody of children they serve.
b. ECE staff should request, and closely inspect, photo identification of anyone they do not recognize picking up a child.
c. ECE programs should know enrolled children's custody status, but getting signed, dated documents is of no benefit.
d. Parents enrolling children in ECE programs are not asked to list emergency contact information for any other adults.

99. Among the following, which is included in expert advice to teachers for interacting with students they perceive as demonstrating problem behaviors?

a. Teachers should consider the function or motivation of a behavior.
b. Teachers should always act on their first impulse, as it is the truest.
c. Teachers should avoid interacting with students outside academics.
d. Teachers should keep extracurricular interests apart from projects.

100. According to the American Association of Educators (AAE) Code of Ethics for Educators, educators do not disclose information (except when required by law) about whom?

a. Students
b. (a) and (c)
c. Colleagues
d. Themselves

Answer Key and Explanations for Test #2

Early Childhood Development and Learning

1. C: Scoring two or more standard deviations (SDs) below the mean (average) on a standardized IQ test is commonly accepted as indicating that a child may have delayed or atypical intellectual development. Thus, one SD (B) is incorrect. On standardized IQ tests used today, one SD = 15 points. Hence, 10 points (A) would not be enough to indicate potentially delayed or atypical intellectual development. Since IQ scores are used to indicate possible delayed/atypical intellectual development, answer choice D is incorrect.

2. B: Children classified as "late talkers" by speech-language pathologists and other developmental specialists have expressive vocabularies (words they speak) of fewer than 50 words. However, this general rule does not mean they will always need therapy (A) to increase their vocabularies. Some children meeting this description will be diagnosed with clinically significant speech, language, and/or hearing problems; others will not. Some are simply "late bloomers" whose expressive vocabularies will catch up in time. Others, however, cannot be assumed to be normal and not needing therapy (C). Parents should thus consult a professional if a child speaks fewer than 50 words at around 18–24 months of age to determine whether a problem exists. However, speaking in "baby talk" at these ages is normal, so parents should not be concerned about imperfect pronunciation in a two-year-old (D).

3. A: Internal consistency reliability means that items that propose to measure the same construct produce similar scores. Parallel forms reliability (B) means that two different forms or versions of the same test yield the same scores when each is given to the same students. Test-retest reliability (C) means that a test will yield similar scores when given to a student and then re-administered to the same student a short time later. Inter-rater reliability (D) means that a test gives the same student similar scores when given at the same time and in the same setting but by different administrators.

4. D: For informal assessments of pre-K classes, teachers can make classroom observations during story or circle times, each observation targeting different skills like math, alphabet knowledge, social-emotional skills, emergent writing, oral language, etc. They can make these observations during both small-group (A) and whole-class (B) activities. They should organize the assessments using around three themes per day (C).

5. B: Indoor and outdoor spaces in EC learning environments should be arranged to allow individual, small-group, and large-group activities. Children's products and other visual elements should be placed at child eye level, not adult (A) when displayed. Spaces should be organized to allow, not prohibit, children's movement among activities (C) without unduly distracting other students. Spaces should also be arranged to promote children's positive social interactions (D) and behaviors, not to prevent these.

6. A: When a screening tool identifies a potential mental health disorder, and then a complete diagnostic evaluation confirms this prediction by diagnosing an actual mental health disorder, the screening tool has demonstrated good predictive validity. An instrument correctly identifying 6 of 10 children *with* developmental disorders or delays is said to have a *sensitivity* of 60%, not specificity (B). An instrument correctly identifying 8 of 10 children *without* disorders or delays has 80% *specificity*, not sensitivity (C). Identification of delays/disorders where none exist constitutes false-*positive* errors (D).

7. A: Children of preschool ages are in Freud's third, Phallic stage of psychosexual development. Freud theorized in this stage, boys undergo the Oedipal conflict; neo-Freudians theorized girls undergo the Electra conflict. In each, children subconsciously fear retaliation from same-sex parents against the child's unconscious desire for opposite-sex parents. Little boys prefer Mommy, little girls Daddy. (In what he termed "identification with the aggressor," Freud/neo-Freudians said children resolve these conflicts by preferring and imitating same-sex parents.) (B) applies Freud's second, Anal stage of development. Making too much of the toilet-training process can result in the child's fixation in this stage. The results are either "anal-retentive" preoccupation with cleanliness, order, and detail; or conversely, "anal-expulsive" rebellion against authority, and/or messy behaviors. (C) applies Freud's first, Oral stage, when nursing babies learn about the world through their mouths. (D) applies Freud's fourth, Latency stage, when children's relationship focus shifts from parents to friends/classmates.

8. B: Instructional objectives are influenced by the major behaviorist learning theory principle that only behaviors that other people can observe and measure can be modified. Hence, in applying Bloom's Taxonomy, such objectives avoid vague internal terms like 'Remember' and 'Understand' (choice A) and instead use only action verbs to describe how students must demonstrate learning (choice B). Choice D is incorrect because it suggests measurability is optional, whereas behaviorism emphasizes observable and measurable behavior.

9. D: The interview method for gathering screening/assessment information from adults about infants and young children can involve brief interviews, but they typically still take longer than paper-and-pencil self-reporting questionnaires, surveys, or checklists. Interviews may be conducted in a structured format using the questions given (A); or in a semi-structured format wherein the administrator uses his/her judgment (B) in adding questions to those published to obtain complete enough information. Interview questions can cover not only the child's identified areas of strengths and needs (C), but also parental concerns, parent-child interactions, the child's behavior, and other subjects.

10. D: Deductive logic, i.e. applying general principles to predict specific instances, only develops fully during the stage of Formal Operations, around 11 years and older. Magical thinking (A) is typical of children in Piaget's Preoperational stage, from around 2-6 years. At this age their thinking is not logical but intuitive (C). Symbolic representation (B) develops near the end of the Sensorimotor stage, at ages around 18-24 months, when children begin to use objects to symbolize other objects during pretend/make-believe play. Inductive logic is the complementary concept to deductive logic. Instead of applying general principles to specific instances, the thinker uses specific instances to draw generalizations. In Piaget's theory, this type of logical reasoning emerges during the concrete operational stage (around 7–11 years), earlier than the more abstract deductive logic of the formal operational stage.

11. C: EC experts say that indoor learning environments for toddlers and preschoolers should have the rooms organized to enable a variety of activities, but not necessarily to limit the activities to certain areas (A). The floors in the rooms should include both hard and carpeted floors (B) to allow crawling, toddling, walking, etc., which should not be limited by insufficient space. Preschool math and science activities might occur in multiple areas of a classroom (D), while the room still should be laid out to facilitate their taking place.

12. B: EC educators should make organized outlines of developmentally applicable guidelines for the children they serve. These outlines provide foundations for the anecdotal observations and authentic assessments they will use to track children's developmental progress; hence they are not unnecessary (A). ECE programs must include ample opportunities and activities for children to develop each individual skill, which includes all of the practice and review they need in order to retain what they learn (C). For tracking children's progress, ECE programs should use systems that follow developmental sequences (D). This helps teachers know whether they can advance some children to the next level, or need to reinforce some previously taught skills for other children.

13. A: Continuous monitoring and charting not only inform teachers of student progress with individual short-term objectives, enabling them to adjust instruction timely as needed; they also give students visual illustrations of their own learning and immediate teacher feedback, not delayed (b). Teachers can also have students make graphs of their own performance and set goals for themselves (c), enhancing student engagement in learning. However, continuous monitoring is not an activity that gives students practice through independent study (d).

14. C: Not all screening and assessment instruments used in EC education programs are appropriate for use with ethnically diverse populations. Depending on their authors and the populations samples used for norming, they may be culturally biased. Screening and assessment instruments used with EC students vary in which developmental domains they measure (A). Different tests are intended for use in different applications (B). The methods of administration also vary across instruments (D).

15. C: In ECE settings, teachers and administrators should create organized outlines containing guidelines for developmentally appropriate practices and outcomes. These should include the schedules and methods for introducing and reinforcing the guidelines at each stage. Based on these outlines, educators can then use authentic assessments, observations, and other means of monitoring children's progress. Lesson plans should not only promote attainment of the developmental guidelines, but also appeal to children's interests (A) to be meaningful. Progress tracking should not only be systematic, but also follow developmental sequences (B). Progress monitoring reveals class and individual levels of performance to inform lesson planning and identify individual children needing added support. Children performing above group level should receive enrichment activities; those performing below group level should receive 1:1 support, rather than vice versa (D).

16. D: Screening instruments are typically more likely to be simpler to score and interpret, often being possible to complete right after administration for sharing with stakeholders. Screening instruments are often used to indicate whether further assessment is needed. Assessment instruments are typically more thorough and involve more complicated scoring and interpretation that take longer. Results and interpretations can be shared with stakeholders later in scheduled meetings. Some techniques common in standardized assessment instruments include interpreting scores by reversing the point values of some items (B); by comparing a student's scores to tables showing the national norms (C) for students of the same age or grade level; and/or converting raw scores (the actual numbers the administrator gave to student responses) to standardized scores or percentages. In contrast, interpreting scores on screening instruments can be as simple as comparing them to a designated cut-off score (D) for further assessment.

17. D: A normally developing three-year-old should be able to tell others his/her name, age, and sex. At two years old (A), a child can usually name familiar objects and speak in short (e.g. two-word) sentences, but cannot always give his/her name, age, and sex yet. A four-year-old (B) typically can do this, as well as use at least four prepositions, identify one or more colors, and repeat four-syllable words s/he hears. A one-year-old (C) typically can use one or more words with correct meaning.

18. D: Formal assessments are typically standardized tests administered to groups of students. They are designed to avoid administrator bias (A) and capture only the children's responses (B). They provide norms for age groups and/or developmental levels for comparison (C). Their data can be scaled and reported in aggregate to school and/or program administrators and policymakers.

19. A: ECE personnel may use formal and/or informal observations to screen and assess children in their populations. Informal observation instruments are less likely to need training for administration (A) and typically occur in natural settings, such as during playtime or daily routines. Formal observations require more training to administer, often involve structured activities, and use standardized protocols to ensure reliable data (B and C). Formal observational instruments often take more time than informal observations (D), averaging more than 20 minutes to administer. Informal observation can take shorter or longer times depending on the observer, child, and activity.

20. C: Responding to simple requests and questions (A) and recognizing nouns that name familiar objects in their environment are characteristics typical of children aged 7-12 months. Wanting to hear the same stories, games, and/or rhymes repeated many times (B) and being able to point at a few of their body parts when asked (D) are characteristic of the language development of children aged 1-2 years. Children typically enjoy hearing stories read or told to them and can answer simple questions about the stories (C) when they are 4-5 years old, so this is the latest development of the choices given.

21. C: According to Roger Brown (1973), a development of his fifth stage, which typically occurs between the ages of 42 and 52 months or older, is the use of the contractible auxiliary verb "to be," as in "They're coming"; and of the contractible copula "to be", as in "She's here." Using the contraction of pronoun and verb form ("s/he's, it's, we're, you're, they're" when "to be" is an auxiliary ("helper") to the verb; and using this contraction when "to be" is the copula/linking verb, i.e. the only verb in the sentence/clause, are developments of Brown's Stage V and not typically found during any of his earlier stages I-IV {(D), (A), (B)}.

22. C: One way that assessment instruments are used in ECE programs is to evaluate the children's achievement of the learning outcomes that define the program's goals (A); and by extension their teachers' effectiveness in furthering their achievement of those outcomes. Assessment tools are also applied to monitor children's progress and other changes over time (B). EC educators also use assessment results for planning curriculum and/or treatment programs (D).

23. B: Children's motor skills normally develop the fastest between the ages of two and six years. By one year, infants usually learn to lift their heads and control their eye muscles; roll over and grasp; sit up and crawl; and stand and creep. They then learn to walk, run, kick, and jump. By three to four years, children can jump up and down and stand on one leg. By five years, they typically can skip, broad-jump, and dress themselves. By six to seven years, they are skillful with throwing, catching, dodging, and directing balls, and they can tie their shoelaces and color pictures.

24. D: Among strategies for effective classroom conflict resolution, experts recommend that teachers have students track conflicts they partake of and/or witness over time; record their observations in journals, but keep the identities of participants anonymous; and then discuss various student reactions to these conflicts that they have observed, including the advantages and disadvantages of each.

25. B: Functional behavior analysis means analyzing a particular behavior to discover what purpose(s) it serves or needs it meets; all behaviors serve a purpose or function. It does not mean analyzing whether a behavior is functional or not (A), or analyzing to what degree it is functional (C). It does not refer to how functional the analysis itself is (D): there is no point in making an analysis unless it works to inform the ensuing behavior modification plan.

26. C: By the age of 6 months (A), babies typically respond to hearing their names; turn their heads and eyes toward human voices; and respond to friendly and angry vocal tones accordingly. By 8 months (B), babies typically utter their first babbling sounds, like a nonspecific "mama," "dada," etc. Children typically say their first true words and can understand and follow simple directions, especially when they are given along with physical and/or vocal cues (C), by the age of 12 months. In the following year they begin making two-word utterances. Children typically have acquired vocabularies of about 5–20 words by 18 months (D). By 24 months, children's vocabularies increase greatly and they may use three-word utterances.

27. A: Kohlberg's Level 1, Preconventional Morality, includes Stage 1, Obedience and Punishment, and Stage 2, Individualism and Exchange. His Level 2, Conventional Morality, includes Stage 3, Interpersonal Relationships (b), and Stage 4, Maintaining Social Order (c). Kohlberg's Level 3, Postconventional Morality, includes Stage 5, Social Contract and Individual Rights (c), (d), and Stage 6, Universal Ethical Principles (d).

28. C: Consistency and repetition are key in early childhood behavior management. Whatever rules adults make, they must always follow them (A); they must repeat them to children many times (B) to make them work; and they must always enforce them consistently (C). Likewise, adults should provide positive reinforcement for good behaviors consistently every time they observe them, not some of the time (D).

29. C: Based on findings of research into conflict resolution in schools, experts recommend role-playing as an effective strategy because it can introduce humor into the conflict resolution process (A); helps students consider the feelings of others (B); teaches them to view behaviors from others' perspectives and empathize with others (C); and promotes more objective examination of conflicts (D) to gain insights about their origins.

30. D: In the most recent revision (Anderson and Krathwohl, 2001), Bloom's Taxonomy follows this sequence: Remember, Understand (a), Apply, Analyze (b), Evaluate, and Create (d). This hierarchy progresses from least to most difficult; hence (c) is incorrect. *(Note: The 2001 revision changed the order, from Synthesis (= Create) and then Evaluation, to Evaluate and then Create, in recognition that the process of synthesizing multiple ideas/sources inherently involves creating new wholes and relationships. It also changed the level names from nouns to verbs.)

31. B: Ordinal position (A) means a child's literal order of birth relative to when his/her siblings were born. Psychological position (B) means a child's role in how s/he interacts with his/her siblings rather than actual order of birth. Adler found psychological position more influential on personality development than ordinal position. He said: "It is not, of course, the child's number in the order of successive births which influences his character, but the situation into which he is born and the way in which he interprets it." Therefore he did not find both ordinal position and psychological position equally important (C); neither did he find no effects (D). He found (B) more influential.

32. D: According to Bloom's Taxonomy, Remembering entails retaining, recognizing, and retrieving facts and other information. Understanding additionally entails locating, identifying, explaining, and discussing information. Applying involves illustrating, demonstrating, and interpreting information and using it for solving problems, etc. Analyzing additionally requires breaking information down into components: categorizing, comparing, contrasting, discriminating, examining, questioning, testing, experimenting with, and criticizing information. Evaluating involves also assessing, appraising, judging, rating, and defending information, and making estimates or predictions based on it. Creating entails proposing, planning, designing, formulating, collecting, developing, composing, organizing, preparing, and managing information.

33. A: In Erikson's theory of psychosocial development, infants from birth to around 18 months learn to develop trust or mistrust in parents' meeting their needs (C) fully and consistently or not. Children aged around 2–3 years, engaged in toilet training and asserting their independence, are developing control over their personal physical skills. Preschoolers aged around 3–5 years, exploring the world around them, are developing and asserting their control over the environment (B). Children beginning school around 6 years old are engaged in learning to form new friendships and other social relationships and learning to address the demands of new tasks at school (D).

34. D: In the early childhood classroom, authentic assessments, such as observations, allow teachers to evaluate individual students' cognitive, physical, social, and emotional development in a natural setting. This allows for a more comprehensive and objective analysis of students' progress toward mastery of particular skills. The data gathered from authentic assessments is beneficial in setting goals for students based upon individual needs, skills, and abilities, as well as influencing future instructional planning.

35. C: Researchers have found that children with "easy" temperaments, who were "easy" babies and are generally easygoing in early childhood, are more likely to keep trying at difficult and/or new tasks, to cope better with feelings of frustration, and to be more willing to tackle challenges. They are NOT more likely to give up upon failing once (A), as children with more "difficult" temperaments are; the latter are also less able to handle challenges and frustration and less likely to persist with repeated attempts (B). Children with "slow to warm up" temperaments (who as babies were initially fretful and fearful of strangers, but given time calmed down and warmed up to people) are likely to become discouraged easily, but given enough encouragement, they learn to keep trying (D).

36. C: Jean Piaget believed that children pass through four distinct developmental stages, with each characterized by increasingly complex skills, abilities, and processes. According to his theory, prekindergarten students are in the preoperational stage of cognitive development. In this stage, young children typically engage in symbolic play as a means of organizing, representing, and understanding both their own thoughts and the world around them. Symbolic play is integral to promoting cognitive, social, emotional, physical, and behavioral development in preoperational children.

37. C: Typically, young children first learn simpler phonemic awareness tasks such as isolating, categorizing, and blending phonemes. The recognition of rhymes is generally learned early on. More advanced skills include segmenting and manipulating phonemes within words.

38. D: While all students progress at individual rates, certain atypical patterns may be indicative of a developmental delay. In this situation, the student's symptoms are characteristic of autism spectrum disorder (ASD). This is a developmental condition that can cause a range of delays across domains. Upon noticing that this student displays atypical behaviors, the teacher must refer the student for an initial evaluation to determine the need for special education services. Doing so will help ensure that this student receives the support necessary to learn effectively.

39. D: Small inner rooms and partitions in indoor environments provide ways for children to experience privacy and solitude when needed. Adult laps for cuddling (A), pillows and soft upholstery (B) and thickly carpeted floor areas (C) are all related to providing for children's sensory needs for softness, but not for privacy.

40. C: Brown (1973) categorized correct use of irregular past tenses of verbs in his Stage III, associated with the age range of 36-42 months. Stage I (A) is associated with Stage I Sentence Types (Operations of Reference subtypes and Semantic Relations subtypes). Stage II (B) is associated with using the present progressive verb tense, regular *–s* plural endings, and the prepositions *in* and *on.* Stage IV (D) is associated with using articles, regular past tenses, and regular present tenses in the third person. Stage V is associated with using third-person irregular verbs, the uncontactable auxiliary form of "to be", the contractible copula form of "to be", and the contractible auxiliary form of "to be".

Content Knowledge and Responsive Teaching Strategies

41. D: To help them build strong oral language skills, adults should include questions in their conversations with young children that require them to form and express abstract concepts to answer. They should use rich vocabulary and complex sentence structures rather than simple ones. They should not just tell young children things but also ask them questions. Adults should not do most of the talking but engage young children in interactive conversations where both contribute equally.

42. B: For preschool-age children, incorporating fine-motor skills activities into play is both more effective and more developmentally appropriate than separating quiet activities from playtime. Tying shoes, stringing beads, and drawing with writing implements develop fine-motor skills, not gross-motor skills. Running, kicking, throwing, and catching balls develop gross-motor skills, not fine-motor skills. Such unstructured exercise is better for preschool-age children than structured games with rules that they are too young to understand or follow.

43. C: Testing a hypothesis requires conducting research, e.g., doing an experiment, making field observations, or administering a survey and analyzing the results. Watching videos (a), reading textbooks (b), and listening to lectures (d)—even while taking notes—are not experiential learning activities because they do not involve hands-on learning activities in which students participate directly. Rather than passively absorbing information, students learn by doing in experiential activities.

44. D: To enhance their shared reading to promote young children's development of vocabulary and oral language, teachers can explain the meanings of new words to them; point at illustrations in books depicting new vocabulary words; connect new vocabulary words to words the children already know; and give children multiple and various examples to teach new vocabulary words. Young children are unlikely to be able to effectively develop their vocabulary and oral language on their own.

45. A: The whole language approach, as its name implies, is holistic in nature and founded on constructivist principles; it supports children in constructing their own knowledge and meaning through interacting with their environments (B). This approach does emphasize the integration of literacy instruction across the various subject content domains (C). It also emphasizes cultural diversity in learners, instruction, and learning (D). However, because it is holistic rather than analytical like phonics, the whole language approach is NOT as effective for children who have language processing disorders and/or reading disorders because they require explicit instruction to learn the decoding skills and strategies that other children learn incidentally as they learn to read and write.

46. A: According to the National Council of Teachers of Mathematics (NCTM)'s standards for students in pre-kindergarten through grade 2, children in this age range should be able to draw upon their experience to identify whether given events are "likely" or "unlikely" to occur. Being able to propose predictions and justify them based on data they gather (B); to collect and analyze data, draw conclusions about the data, and justify those conclusions using those data (C); and to design studies to investigate inferences or predictions they make (D) are all standards that the NCTM designates for students in grades 3 through 5.

47. A: On a test designed to measure a particular construct, such as intelligence, that has a varied assortment of questions, tasks, or stimuli within the instrument to measure different aspects, they should still all be aspects of the same construct for the test to have internal consistency. However, in comprehensive tests that cover multiple domains, one should not expect internal consistency among its subscales (B) that evaluate different domains of development, e.g., gross motor skills vs. language skills. Also, in such multi-domain tests, one should not expect internal consistency between each of the domains tested and the test's full-scale or overall score (C). However, if children with different developmental needs receive similar scores on the same test through their responses to different test items (D), that may be a sign that the test has low internal consistency.

48. B: Kinesthetic activities are those in which the individual learns to understand abstract concepts and relationships through touching various textures, manipulating solid objects, and engaging in physical actions and movements like dance and sports. A visual activity is one in which the individual understands and learns through looking at visible and colorful illustrations, graphics, and objects. An auditory activity is one in which the individual learns through listening to music, spoken language, and other sounds. Concrete does not usually refer to a type of activity.

49. B: Teachers should first review national and state standards, course textbooks, additional materials, and required test preparation materials; create a plan of study; plan instructional units and timelines; make a personal lesson plan calendar; and then write detailed lesson plans within each unit. They should not write lesson plans before making a calendar (A) or planning their timelines (C) for covering each unit, since these will affect the lesson plans. Writing lesson plans before planning units (D) makes no sense, as the lesson plans are components of the units.

50. A: The cephalocaudal principle means that growth and development progress from the head downward: babies gain control over their heads before the rest of their bodies. The proximodistal principle means that growth and development also progress from the center of the body outward: babies gain control of their torsos before their extremities.

51. B: When preschool teachers prompt children to use different body postures and movements to portray various emotions, the children do get appreciable physical exercise (A); learn ways to express emotions (B) in ways that are concrete so they can understand them and reinforce them through a physical connection; and, while having fun (C) and using creative thinking (D).

52. D: Interactive learning activities emphasize the sharing, exchange, and discussion of ideas, questions, activities, tasks, and learning among students. Indirect instruction (a) overlaps with interactive learning in discussion, for example. Independent study (b) overlaps with interactive learning in certain cooperative learning group exercises. Experiential learning (c) overlaps with interactive learning in role-playing activities.

53. D: Math education experts believe that when children can count to twenty, thirty, etc., to one hundred, they begin to discover the first consistent mathematical pattern they observe, that of base ten (i.e., twenty = two tens, thirty = three tens, etc., and we add only numbers from one to nine before reaching the next set of tens). Learning to count from one to twelve involves memorization, but NOT more unusual rules (A). Counting from thirteen to nineteen *does* involve less regular rules, in addition to the same amount of memorizing, NOT more (B). However, learning to count above twenty actually involves *more* consistent rules (C), and these facilitate children's recognition of the base ten pattern.

54. B: Younger children are more likely to respond to specific word prompts in terms of their typical sequence in sentences, e.g., "dog – barks," "eat – lunch," whereas when they grow older, they typically respond to specific word prompts in terms of their parts of speech, with a related word that is the same part of speech, e.g., "dog – cat," "eat – drink" (A). Choices C and D each combine one linguistic characteristic of younger children with one of older children.

55. C: According to Head Start, adults should let young children choose among activities and when to switch to others, not choose for them (A). Young children are capable of this. Adults can create several "play stations", e.g., throwing a ball at a target; throwing a ball into a floor hoop; rolling a ball at a target; jumping over boxes on the floor; and jumping through floor hoops. Adults should use not only words, but also physical demonstrations of physical activities (B) divided into steps. This clarifies the physical actions involved, and also helps children who learn more visually than verbally (this is not only a matter of learning modality; it is also common in early childhood to learn via visual observation when language skills are less developed). Adults should provide open-ended and simple activities so children of any skill level can succeed (C). Young children's short attention spans mean they should be given frequent changes and variety in activities (D).

56. C: Students frequently want to know how they will use academic content in their lives before engaging in it. To meet this need, teachers should give them many different examples (a) and explain what preparation the content will give them for future opportunities. Students also often need to discover underlying principles independently (b), which teachers can enable by providing problems students must reason through, affording opportunities for mastery. Teachers can make cooperative learning effective through positive social pressure (d).

57. C: Teaching young children the notion of time, continuity, and change is necessary to develop their understanding of foundational concepts related to social studies, such as cause and effect, as well as how to accurately situate, recall, and make connections between historical events. Doing so should take place in a developmentally appropriate, familiar, and applicable context to ensure understanding. In this situation, labeling the days of the week as "yesterday," "today," and "tomorrow," as well has having students locate various events on a monthly calendar, shows how time functions in their daily lives. This strategy helps students begin to understand that time is linear and events happen chronologically, developing their sense of time, continuity, and change.

58. C: Introducing new concepts in science using active learning opportunities to promote exploration, creativity, and observation fosters students' natural sense of curiosity in the early childhood classroom. Doing so strengthens students' connections to learning by encouraging them to ask questions and test ideas, and helping them process new information. By having students create bird feeders to hang outside and observe, this teacher uses a hands-on learning approach to introduce the concept that animals have basic needs. This strategy will encourage students to watch as birds come to eat from the feeders they created, establishing a real-world foundation for understanding that living animals require food for survival.

59. A: Teachers can obtain a good assessment of the level of print awareness a young child has developed by using a storybook, so option B is incorrect. The teacher should first ask a young child to identify the front, back, spine, and title of the book; this is not unnecessary, unlike answer C suggests, because some children with undeveloped/less developed print awareness may not know these things or where to start reading a book. Unlike what answer D suggests, just because a child demonstrates a level of print awareness while reading a storybook does not mean the child is ready to move on to reading novels independently. Teachers should also ask children to identify punctuation marks, uppercase letters, and lowercase letters. Teachers should not only praise children's correct responses; they should also correct wrong responses and review the corrections.

60. A: Effective instructional planning in science is based on a set of central unifying themes within the field. This promotes student learning and development in science by establishing a foundation for understanding increasingly complex ideas while demonstrating the connections between scientific concepts. In this situation, students will learn that liquid takes the shape of its container by transferring water from a cup to a bowl, and then to a tray, thus developing a fundamental understanding of the law of conservation of matter. This law applies to the unifying concept of constancy and change; it states that although matter can change shape and form, its quantity remains constant.

61. D: Recognizing the characteristics and functions of English grammatical conventions is important for reading comprehension development. Further, modeling to students how these patterns apply to spoken language is necessary for fostering reading fluency and expressive language skills. By pausing between sentences, changing intonation, and correlating inflection with variances in punctuation within the text, the teacher effectively models the relationship between English grammatical patterns in written and spoken language.

62. B: Early childhood experts advise that teachers can and should find science teaching materials in their everyday environments, which cost nothing and appeal to children's natural curiosity and interests. Preschool children do not learn best from textbooks (A), even age-appropriate books; they enjoy learning with real-world materials. For example, found objects from nature like rocks, loose bird feathers, fallen leaves, etc. make good science materials (C). Teachers can also obtain animal fur from local groomers and turtle shells, snakeskins, etc. from local pet stores (D) as useful teaching materials.

63. D: By "private speech", Vygotsky meant the way that young children typically verbalize aloud to themselves while engaging in solitary activities. This helps them to think through their actions; make decisions; solve problems; and strengthen their knowledge of the correct sequences in activities with multiple steps. In using the term "private speech," Vygotsky was not referring to a private conversation with another child (A) or an adult (B); or silent mental speech (C)—which Vygotsky termed "inner speech." He said that children eventually internalized their external private speech: it progressed from overtly speaking aloud to oneself, to mentally speaking silently to oneself. Both private and inner speech serve the same functions at different ages.

64. C: Puppet shows are not only entertaining but are also concrete ways to engage young children in viewing and then discussing demonstrations of desirable/undesirable social behaviors. Since motor skills develop before verbal skills, many preschoolers use physical aggression to get what they want instead of expressing themselves verbally. A puppet show depicting the failures of aggressive actions and successes of verbal communication can couch instructive content in a fun format. For preschool ages, teachers should ask children which puppets were good and which were bad; this does not encourage being judgmental but simply helps children define socially acceptable and unacceptable behaviors. For the same reason, it is not irrelevant to ask children which puppets they liked and disliked. Young children can not only summarize what happened during the show, they also can and should be encouraged to predict what could happen next and how puppet characters could behave differently to exercise and enhance their social understanding and interactions.

65. B: Inventive spelling occurs when students employ their knowledge of letter-sound relationships to spell unfamiliar words. As spelling development occurs in stages, it is important to recognize that many young children will rely on inventive spelling as they begin learning to write. Encouraging this practice has students use their sense of phonemic awareness to sound out new words, ultimately improving their spelling abilities. However, the teacher must correct misspelled words to ensure proper development. Students that continue to use inventive spelling past the normal developmental stage may require additional support and intervention.

66. B: In applying research data showing effectiveness for increasing student achievement, teachers praise students for achieving specific goals (a); use multimodal instruction because students learn and think more and better when they combine linguistic and non-linguistic systems (b); assign homework, which research finds effective along with in-class practice for increasing achievement (c); and have students form and test hypotheses, which aids both critical thinking and achievement (d).

67. C: Word families are words that are spelled and pronounced similarly. For example, the words "brain," "rain," "stain," and "train" all share the "-ain" ending, and therefore belong to the same word family. Introducing word families using the concept of onset and rime—the beginning and ending sounds of a syllable—familiarizes students with the different parts of words. The onset is the initial consonant that begins the syllable, and the rime consists of the remaining vowels and consonants. Teaching this concept first contributes to developing the phonological awareness skills necessary for decoding written language. Doing so helps students identify words in the same word family while promoting vocabulary acquisition, word recognition, and ultimately, reading comprehension skills.

68. C: Promoting students' ability to think algebraically in early elementary school establishes a foundation for thinking abstractly when working with increasingly advanced mathematical concepts. To achieve this, teachers should introduce math experiences gradually as students develop mastery. This method allows young children to progress through increasingly complex levels of algebraic thinking as they learn, while also demonstrating that the same expression can be presented in multiple ways. When introducing a new mathematical concept, teachers should begin by doing so concretely, then pictorially, and ultimately, in abstract terms. For example, in this situation, the teacher could begin by having students work with manipulatives as they solve addition problems, then present the equation using pictures of familiar objects, and eventually, show them only the numerical equation. Doing so helps students learn how to think algebraically when approaching new mathematical concepts.

69. B: By modeling how to create a pattern using beads and providing a hands-on learning experience, the teacher implements age-appropriate and meaningful instruction. In asking open-ended questions as students work, the teacher effectively promotes inquiry and challenges students to employ logical reasoning skills to explain their choice in beads. This strategy also supports the development of students' language skills by encouraging them to elaborate upon their thought processes.

70. A: Thematic units refer to instructional activities across the curriculum that focus on a particular topic. In the early childhood classroom, this approach allows students to explore a new concept in-depth by engaging in various related learning activities. Regarding scientific learning and development, thematic units strengthen understanding by integrating new concepts into daily learning activities while demonstrating the connection between science and other content areas. In this thematic unit, students will explore the features of space by participating in literacy, art, and music activities.

71. B: In children's literature, picture books represent both a genre (A), a type of book, and a format (C) that includes other different genres within it. For example, picture books can be fictional or nonfiction, narrative or expository, prose or poetry, traditional or modern, etc. Wordless storybooks have only pictures and no text; picture books have pictures and text integrated interdependently; and illustrated storybooks have primarily text, with secondary but complementary and usually plentiful pictures. Hence picture books represent both genre and format, so their representing neither (D) is incorrect.

72. B: An activity using non-standard measures to compare something like the weight of apples and grapes is helpful in learning inference skills, since students have to try out different combinations to find the balance. Students improve their inference skills by using the outcome of one attempt to inform their next through inference. Observation skills are also exercised in activities like these, as the students have to observe and operate the scales to find their answer, but it is not such a observationally focused activity as studying and describing physical traits of different objects. Communication would be a key feature if this type of activity were used in a group. Classification is not particularly exercised in this type of activity, since the only classifications would be the type of fruit, which is a given in this type of activity.

73. C: Fine motor skills are purposeful, coordinated small-muscle movements, specifically using the fingers, hands, and wrists. These skills are needed for a variety of daily tasks, so early childhood educators must offer several materials and activities to develop them. While individual children progress at varying rates, most kindergarten students can reasonably be expected to begin using tools such as pencils, crayons, and paintbrushes with a degree of purpose and control. By incorporating these materials of varying sizes into the art section of the classroom, this teacher effectively promotes students' mastery of fine motor skills while recognizing and accommodating individual ability levels.

74. A: Scientific learning and development are best supported when young children are provided with hands-on learning experiences that promote their natural curiosity. Such activities allow for active exploration in which students use their physical senses for investigation and inquiry, fostering engagement and strengthening understanding of how scientific concepts apply to the world around them. By leading a class nature walk to introduce the characteristics of living and nonliving things, students have the opportunity to physically touch, smell, observe, and listen as they begin exploring the characteristics of living and nonliving things in nature. This ultimately places the new concept in a relevant and meaningful context for young students, providing a framework for greater understanding when the unit begins.

75. A: Patterns are any actions, events, movements, images, sounds, numbers, etc., that are regularly repeated. Relationships are logical or reasoned associations among things. Awareness and understanding of patterns and relationships allow children to understand how objects and concepts are categorized into groups and how rhythm works (in music, dance, poetry, speech, art, etc.), as well as how to order things, like from smallest to biggest. Being aware of and comprehending patterns and relationships not only support children's understanding of the structures of things in reality but also allow them to predict events before they occur because of the regularity of repetition in patterns and the logic in relationships. Patterns and relationships exist in geometry, algebra, other branches of mathematics, art, and music. Research has shown that children with strong pattern understanding usually have strong executive function skills. While pattern recognition can be practiced and taught in a classroom, children naturally begin to identify patterns at a young age independent of deliberate instruction.

76. D: Five stages of spelling identified (Gentry, 1982) are: Precommunicative; Semiphonetic; Phonetic; Transitional; and Correct. In the Phonetic stage, children represent all the speech sounds they hear in words with written letters. While their spelling in this stage is not always correct, it is nonetheless applied systematically and understandable to others. Children in the fifth, Correct (A) stage usually spell words accurately and recognize misspellings. In the fourth, Transitional (B) stage, children begin moving from using phonetic spellings to conventional ones. In the second, Semiphonetic (C) stage, children are just beginning to represent sounds with corresponding letters. (In the first, Precommunicative stage, children may use alphabet letters, but do not yet show understanding of letter-sound correspondences.)

77. B: It is both more effective and more developmentally appropriate for preschool-aged children to incorporate motor activities into playtime than to separate play from quiet activities (A). EC teachers can help children develop fine-motor skills by playing indoors with crayons, tying shoelaces, and using other small objects, and outdoors on nature walks by picking up pebbles and twigs, and throwing them into streams or ponds to develop both small and large muscles as well as coordination. Structured games with rules (C) are too difficult for most preschoolers to understand or follow. Instead of formal ball games, EC teachers can have them kick, throw, and catch balls as more unstructured exercise. Running, skipping, and playing tag are more appropriate for developing preschoolers' large muscle skills than more complicated games. Motor activities for preschool-aged children should be planned for shorter times because their short attention spans will not accommodate longer durations (D).

78. A: Maintaining regular communication with students' families is integral to fostering the sense of partnership necessary for productive collaboration. Doing so helps to ensure that families feel informed and included in the learning and assessment process, thereby encouraging their active participation. Such a relationship allows teachers and families to effectively work together to find strategies, approaches, and resources to enhance students' learning and development.

79. D: Teaching young children to make predictions is an effective strategy for supporting their learning and development related to probability, as it encourages students to consider the likelihood of potential outcomes. This establishes a foundation of understanding that can later be applied to more advanced mathematical situations that involve determining probability. Further, representing students' predictions using a bar graph promotes the understanding that information can be quantified and represented in visual form, which supports learning and development in data analysis.

80. D: EC teachers can assign children to small groups to make class rules and then to revise them to be more realistic. For example, children might make a rule of "No talking" and then revise it to say "Listen when others talk" or "Speak softly in class." EC teachers need not limit their materials to non-fiction; creative teachers have successfully illustrated citizenship concepts via children's literature (A). This is effective because children personally identify with story characters, and the situations in the stories are cognitively appropriate for making citizenship concepts concrete and real to children (B). Fictional narratives can also serve as springboards for starting discussions with young children about when rules do or do not apply. This method can often engage their interest and comprehension more than simply reading actual rules (C).

Professionalism and Collaborative Partnerships

81. D: Because of danger and liability issues, giving medication to children in ECE settings is controversial but often necessary. ECE staff should label children's medications with drug name, child's name, doctor's name and contact information, and dosage and administration instructions to prevent errors. ECE centers/programs must write and follow policies and procedures observing their state government's licensing requirements for medical care and treatment (A). ECE experts advise centers/programs require doctor and parent permission for giving children any prescription/non-prescription medication (B). In addition to keeping written parental consent on file, centers/programs should post separate charts for easy staff access with the child's name, medication, dosage, time to administer, and teacher initials. This does not induce redundancy or errors (C); rather, it documents that teachers follow physicians' and parents' directions, and can prevent errors.

82. B: One issue affecting ECE facilities is if state authorities remove a child from the parents' custody. Another issue that does affect ECE facilities is if two parents not living together are pursuing child custody (C) because parents frequently demand to visit with or take the child home even when they do not have custody, so ECE personnel must know this. Answer choice A describes the definition of physical custody, not legal custody. Answer choice D is the definition of legal custody, not physical custody. Physical custody does not confer all the rights of full legal custody.

83. B: Title I, Part A is a federally funded program intended to help close the achievement gap for economically disadvantaged students. This program allocates more financial assistance to schools with a high percentage of students from low-income households to provide the support necessary to facilitate equitable learning opportunities. Funds may be used to provide learning materials and resources, additional staff, intervention programs, and staff development opportunities. In addition, Title I funds may be used to give families access to resources and education to further support their children's learning and development.

84. B: Developing culturally competent practices in the classroom requires the teacher to recognize and work to eliminate personal biases and assumptions about other cultures. In doing so, the teacher gains appreciation for and strengthens understanding of individual students' backgrounds, beliefs, traditions, and values. This allows the teacher to make more informed decisions to design more thoughtful, relevant, and inclusive instruction that meets the needs of all students. In addition, working to develop culturally competent and globally aware teaching practices communicates to students that their diversities are valued and respected, encouraging them to adopt the same sentiment toward others and improving the overall classroom climate.

85. C: Head Start is a federally funded education program designed to help close the achievement gap by providing an equitable foundation for learning and development among prekindergarten students from socioeconomically disadvantaged backgrounds. This program also provides information and resources to families to help support their children in promoting healthy development and learning.

86. D: Communicating high expectations of students to parents makes them allies, and enables parents to reinforce teacher expectations at home. Research finds parental expectations strongly predict student achievement. Teachers should communicate about the whole class, not just parents' own children (B). This enables parents to see teachers' viewpoints about decisions not ideal for individual students but best for the group. Teachers should ask parents which communication methods they prefer, and use these (C). They should measure results like parental participation, student preparation, and which methods elicit the highest student and parent responses, adjusting communication plans accordingly (D).

87. B: PDCs work with new teachers and their mentors to ensure teachers' PD goals meet school district guidelines. They do sometimes pay workshop tuition, so answer A is wrong. They also provide documentation for state licensure boards of new teachers' efforts to meet state requirements by approving the teachers' PD plans (PDPs). They collaborate with school district administrators in setting both interdisciplinary and subject-specific, district-wide professional teacher goals, so options C and D are wrong.

88. C: Experts report that reflective teachers have no fear of either self-evaluation (a) or evaluation by others (b), but rather want their self-improvement efforts to be informed by feedback from other experienced educators (c) and are motivated to improve mainly to serve their students best rather than to receive better appraisals (d).

89. A: Teacher participation in committees, projects, and other school functions affords more opportunities for teachers to pursue professional development. School rules and disciplinary procedures are often decided in these functions as well. They also provide leadership for intramural and other athletic events, training in individual content-area subjects, tutoring and contribute to fundraising efforts and crisis management programs. Participation in committees, projects, and school functions is, therefore, not generally a waste of time. Participation in sporting events is not usually required.

90. C: Learning communities are a type of PD that enables educators not only to share information but also to collaborate on producing presentations, workshops, etc. Mentors help educators develop PD plans; observe and give feedback; share knowledge, expertise, and experience; and give support. Study groups enable information exchange like learning communities but not presentations and workshops. Pre-service internships give educators close on-the-job supervision, practice, and work experience.

91. A: National Education Association is a labor union for educators. The other answer choices are professional organizations but not labor unions.

92. D: One way teachers can participate in school or district projects, committees, and activities is by contributing to curriculum design and text identification and adoption (D). Teachers can contribute to a great number of discussions and decisions beyond those taking place in faculty, department, staff, and PTA/PTO meetings (A). For example, teachers are well-equipped to serve as members of committees tasked with deciding on special population admissions, reviews, and dismissals (C). Teachers, students, administrators, and others may all benefit from the individual expertise and special interest knowledge teachers contribute (B).

93. B: Teacher performance appraisal systems evaluate not only whether a teacher's instruction is effective, but also whether it is student-centered (a); whether students participate actively and successfully in their learning (b); whether teachers not only evaluate student progress regularly, but also give students feedback (c) based on these progress evaluations; and not only on the time, materials, and instructional strategies that teachers use, but also their management of student discipline (d).

94. A: Students have difficulty learning, and educators have difficulty working, in school environments as inadequate and distracting as the examples described. Although riots in school seem more serious due to violence and safety issues, other school environmental factors like those described, while less dramatic, are equally important (b) to teaching and learning. Although sufficiently motivated students may learn in less than ideal environments, many will learn less, less well, or find learning impossible when school environmental factors interfere enough (c). School factors, home factors, and community factors all affect teaching learning in different ways; one is not more important than another (d).

95. C: Legally, ECE centers are responsible for the welfare of children on their premises. If parents do not pick up their child and much time has elapsed, ECE staff are *less* likely to incur legal liability if they keep the child at the center (A) and *more* likely to incur legal liability if they take the child home with them (B). If it is impossible for staff and child to stay at the center and staff must remove a child who was left, the staff *should* inform the police (D) they are doing so and where they are taking the child to protect themselves from potential liability. If parents exhibit a chronic pattern of being tardy picking up their children, ECE staff must talk with them about why and what solutions are possible (C) because ECE employees are legally responsible to report it if they suspect child neglect.

96. A: Technology enables teachers to communicate with parents in a variety of ways, such as email, text messaging, Facebook messages/posts, X posts, posts on class/school websites, and videoconferencing. Teachers can save a lot of time and effort using word-processing software programs to create learning units and lesson plans. They can read and grade papers and also add comments. For example, MS Word has a comments area in the right margin, and Adobe Acrobat PDFs allow adding comments as electronic sticky notes. Though some texts can be found online for free, this is not the case for all texts, and these may be illegal copies. While technology can aid instruction, no technology replaces instruction.

97. D: Principle II, Ethical Conduct toward Practices and Performance of the AAE Code of Ethics, includes not misrepresenting official school policies and distinguishing these from personal opinions. Principle I, Ethical Conduct toward Students (A), concerns educator interaction with students and protecting student information, not school policies. Principle III, Ethical Conduct toward Professional Colleagues (B), concerns educator interaction with and protecting information of colleagues. Principle IV, Ethical Conduct toward Parents and Community (C), concerns educator interactions with students' parents and communities.

98. B: Any time an adult whom the staff member(s) do(es) not recognize comes to pick up a child from an ECE facility, the staff should request photo identification of that person and closely inspect it. ECE program administrators are not legally authorized to make any decisions about the legal or physical custody of children their program serves (A). ECE program personnel should not just know every enrolled child's custody status; they should procure and keep on file a signed and dated document for each child indicating the child's custody status, names, contact information, and the relationships of all adults authorized to pick up the child (C), and copies of any separation agreements and/or court decisions. Parents enrolling children in ECE programs are always asked to list emergency contact information for other adults (D).

99. A: Experts advise teachers to change their own behavior if they want student behavior to change. Rather than acting on their first impulse in response to problem behaviors—which has not worked if the behaviors persist—experts advise teachers to stop and consider the function or motivation of a behavior, which can include securing the teacher's attention or simply connecting with the teacher. Teachers can eliminate the need for problem behaviors by giving students what they need in more appropriate ways. Expert advice also includes interacting with students in non-academic games or activities that students choose and observing their strengths and interests. Teachers are also advised to assign individual and group projects enabling students to express their extracurricular interests through their preferred media.

100. B: The AAE Code of Ethics for Educators specifically names students (a) and professional colleagues (c) as those whose information educators should not disclose unless required by law. It does not specify that educators should protect the confidentiality of information about the educators themselves (d) or about parents, community members, or others.